Benson's Ride Through History:

1880 - 1945

Benson, Arizona

Mary Lee Tiernan

Copyright ©2021 by Mary Lee Tiernan.

All rights reserved. No portion of this product may be photographed, scanned, translated, reproduced, copied, or reduced to any tangible or electronic medium or machine-readable form, without the prior written consent of Mary Lee Tiernan. Contact mlt@maryleetiernan.com

ISBN 978-0983067283

First Paperback Edition June 2021

Cover photo courtesy of Bob Nilson

www.maryleetiernan.com

Acknowledgements

I thank all the people who shared information and/or photographs used in this book. There are many of you. In particular, I thank the following organizations and individuals for their support:

Church of Jesus Christ of Latter-Day Saints in Pomerene, AZ, for the use of their library.

San Pedro Valley Arts and Historical Society, Benson, AZ. Photos used in this book with the credit "Courtesy San Pedro Valley Arts & Historical Society" were acquired with permission to use when the museum functioned under that name and Director Cheryl Mammano. In 2017, the museum was renamed the Benson Historical Museum.

Edward Ellsworth
Bob Nilson
Gerry Thomson

Many of the photographs used in the book are not of the best quality because they are 100-years-old or more. The originals had yellowed, been scratched or torn, and were fuzzy. I "cleaned" them as best I could in Photoshop but did not change the content. Given a choice between including flawed images or not using them at all, I chose to use them. Photos without attribution are my personal property.

Table of Contents

Chapter 1	From Desert to Town	7
Chapter 2	The Mysterious Mr. Benson	19
Chapter 3	Benson's Neighbors	27
Chapter 4	Bad Boys..	37
Chapter 5	The 1880s: Growing Up	55
Chapter 6	The 1890s: Becoming Civilized	73
Chapter 7	The 1900s: Hitting the Heights	89
Chapter 8	The 1910s: Reinventing Itself	105
Chapter 9	The 1920s: Prosperity	127
Chapter 10	The 1930s: A Time to Mourn	147
Chapter 11	Hang on, Cowboy	179
Chapter 12	The 1940s: Clouds of War	189
Endnotes	....	219
Bibliography	....	227

Chapter 1

From Desert to Town

1877, 1878, 1879, 1880: the ribbon of steel stretched farther and farther eastward across the Southwest desert. A good day yielded two more miles of track. Slowly but steadily, Southern Pacific Railroad laid track from California through the Arizona and New Mexico Territories on its way to connect with the Texas and Pacific Railway in El Paso, Texas. When the two railroads met, the rails would form one continuous line from coast to coast along the southern United States.

On June 14th, 1880, workers toiling under the blazing desert sun reached the San Pedro Valley located in the eastern side of the Arizona Territory where the grade dipped down to the site chosen for crossing the San Pedro River. By the first week of July, they had erected a bridge across the river and added three more miles of track eastward. The workers would continue on but leave behind a new town.

The dream of uniting the nation by rail was finally underway. The United States Federal Government had conducted five surveys between 1853 and 1855 to find the best routes across the United States for transcontinental railroads. Plans for building the railroad, however, were postponed because of the Civil War. After the war, the nation focused once again on joining the east and west coasts by rail.

The first transcontinental railroad opened for through traffic on May 10, 1869, amid much fanfare when the Central Pacific and Union Pacific lines connected San Francisco, California, to Iowa and the existing eastern rail networks. This first route was roughly midway between the nation's northern and southern borders. The second transcontinental rail route first connected with the eastern rail network to Los Angeles, California, on March 8, 1881, when the Southern Pacific met a branch line of the Atchison, Topeka & Santa Fe Railway in Deming in the Territory of New Mexico. The branch line took passengers north to the mainline which ran roughly to Chicago, Illinois, and points east from Los Angeles, California. The Southern Pacific did not finish its project in Deming. From Deming, it continued laying more track east to El Paso, Texas. It followed the southernmost east/west route mapped by the federal surveyors to connect with the Texas and Pacific Railway which ran directly east through Texas, completing the southern transcontinental route.

Laying railroad tracks across the desert. Exact location unknown. Courtesy San Pedro Valley Arts & Historical Society.

Before the connections to other railroads, however, the Southern Pacific had to finish laying tracks across the Arizona Territory and cross the San Pedro River. The site designated as the best place to cross the river was just south of the crossing once used by the Butterfield Overland Stagecoach Company. The Butterfield line had been discontinued 19 years earlier in 1861, but stagecoaches and wagons traveling east or west still used the old Butterfield route and crossing.

On the west side of the river near the crossing, Southern Pacific planned a town. The site sat at the northern end of the San Pedro Valley which had functioned as a natural north/south corridor for centuries, since the time of the earliest indigenous peoples. It was an ideal intersection for a town to service the ranches that dotted the landscape to the north and south. Cattle brought to yards in Benson to be shipped by train would eliminate the need for long cattle drives to the mid-West.

The new town would also serve the new mining operations in the area. Three years before the arrival of the railroad, Ed Schiefflin had discovered silver in Tombstone. Miners flocked to the area and filed numerous claims for their own share of the wealth. The mining companies needed to move out the vast amounts of ore taken from the mines. Once the ore was processed and taken by wagon to the new town, the bullion could easily be shipped east or west to market. The railroad could also more efficiently deliver the supplies needed by the mining and milling operations. The mining industry was about to explode with the discovery of copper in Bisbee as well as minerals in smaller mines all around the area. The ranches and mines needed the railroad, and the railroad wanted their business.

In anticipation of the railroad's arrival, Southern Pacific used the Pacific Improvement Company to plat a town to be named Benson. Railroad magnates C. P. Huntington, Leland Stanford, Mark Hopkins, and Charles Crocker formed the Pacific Improvement Company, a California based holding company, in 1878. The company bought and sold land as well as different types of companies. The company laid out the new town on a northwest/southeast axis with the railroad bisecting the town on the west side of 4th Street.

The plat map, completed in April 1880, showed a rough square comprised of 160 acres. Six avenues ran east and east. Pacific Improvement named them after principal mountain

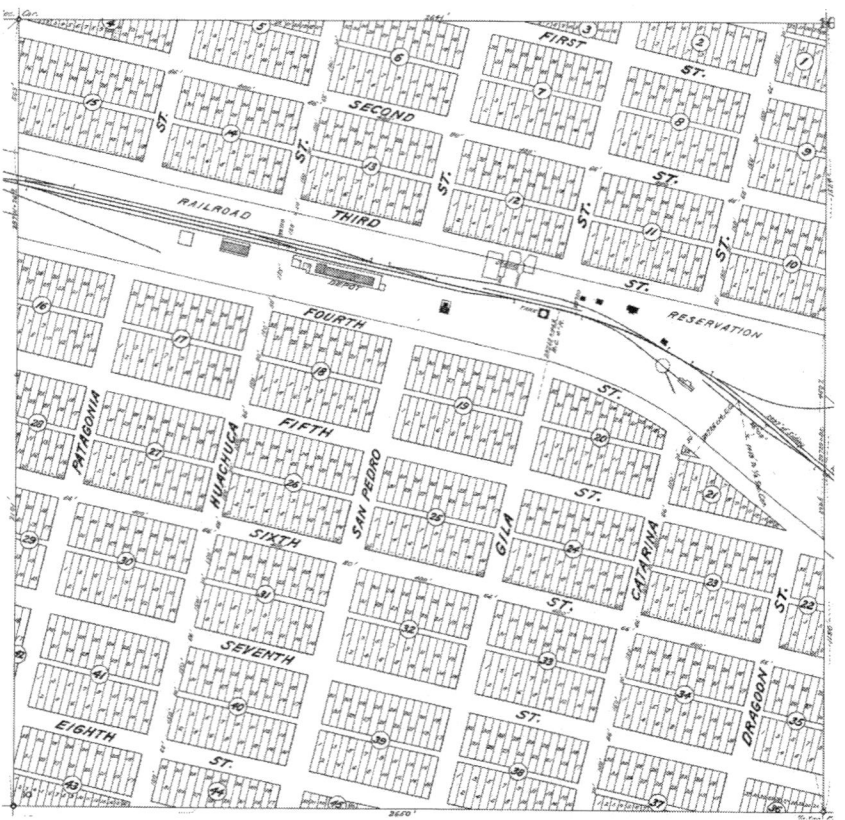

Pacific Improvement's 1884 plat map of Benson. Each full square or block contains approximately 32 lots. Courtesy Bob Nilson.

ranges and rivers in Arizona: Patagonia, Huachuca, San Pedro, Gila, Catarina, and Dragoon. Streets numbered one through eight crossed the avenues, paralleling the tracks on both the north and south sides. An alley ran through the center of each block to allow a back entrance to each lot. The town would not expand much beyond this original plat for the next two decades.

Within a week of the tracks reaching Benson, Southern Pacific started regularly scheduled train service to and from the Pacific Coast for both passengers and freight. Trains cut both travel time and costs. To go from Yuma to Tucson, for example, cost a passenger $22.90 and took one day by train. The same trip on a stagecoach cost $60 and took four days. Shipping freight by train cost about one-third the price of shipping by freight wagon and took one to two days instead of 20.

Although settlers had come to the valley or passed through in small numbers before construction of a railway, those numbers increased dramatically after completion of the transcontinental railroad. The railroad truly opened the land for settlement. Trains provided safer passage into the region because they were not as prone to the Indian and highwayman attacks that plagued stagecoaches and wagons. And the swiftness of train travel shortened the otherwise grueling journey. People came for many reasons. Some came for their health and the dry climate; some for adventure or opportunity or a new start in life; some to escape the crowded conditions in Eastern cities or to dodge the law. Many came to find their fortunes mining the riches hidden in the bowels of the earth. Benson remained the terminus for train service until the end of the summer in 1880.

In the Fall, the train brought a most notable passenger. United States President Rutherford B. Hayes visited Benson and Tucson in October 1880. The *Weekly Arizona Citizen* applauded his visit. "...President Hayes was the first Chief Executive who ever crossed the continent from ocean to ocean. The importance of our vast resources, our great industries and our needs will be better understood, and cannot but further the legislation needed to foster and advance our interests."[1]

A railroad generated a demand for retail trade and services. Passengers needed food and a place to stay during layovers or maybe a telegraph office or even a haircut. When ranchers, farmers, and miners brought their wares to town to be shipped, they needed to stock up on supplies for the return trip. They also wanted a place to take a break from their labors and relax. The shopkeepers and their families who provided the goods and services had needs of their own for everyday living. The town needed hotels, restaurants, markets selling food for man and beast, stores selling general supplies, clothing, or building materials, and an array of specialty services such as a barber, blacksmith, or launderer.

On June 21st, a week after the railroad reached the San Pedro River, the Pacific Improvement Company began selling lots to the public. It ran an excursion train into town and sold from the rear platform. A lot 25 feet wide by 150 feet deep sold for an average of $177. "Terms of Sale: One-third cash on day of sale, balance in six months and twelve months, with interest at the rate of one percent per month on deferred payments."[2] Many of the lots on 4th Street sold first. Their location across the street from the tracks and depot targeted 4th Street as prime commercial real estate.

Entrepreneurs not only bought lots, but some had their businesses up and running very quickly. The *Weekly Arizona Citizen* reported on July 10th that the "Town is very lively just now, and already there are thought to be about 300 people there, while a hotel, three restaurants, six or seven saloons, five or six stores, and two livery stables are doing a 'land-office business.' This growth was nearly all accomplished inside of two weeks."[3] Having actual buildings was a step-up from mining towns like Tombstone and Bisbee which started as 'tent cities.' Benson had the advantage of the train bringing building materials right to its doorstep.

The railroad not only divided Benson in half geographically but socially and economically as well. Soot and odors and clouds of black smoke billowed from the steam locomotives as they huffed and puffed their way up the steep grade out of Benson. With prevailing winds coming from the south/southwest, the emissions would usually blow north/northeast. So the south side of the tracks, with the winds blowing pollution away from it, was the preferable place to be. It would develop as the more

Larger, better-constructed homes were built on the south side of the railroad tracks. Fences kept the cattle out.

A south-side Craftsman bungalow. Homes similar to the above were often built from Sears kits. Owners bought the plans and precut materials and constructed the houses themselves.

desirable part of town. Most middle and upper-class homes, businesses, churches, professional offices, and public facilities such as a hospital, library, city hall, post office, and cemeteries would be built south of the tracks.

On the north side of the tracks, housing accommodated railroad workers and their families. Generally, these structures were quite small. 3rd Street between San Pedro and Huachuca became the "railroad district." Railroad crews and settlers were a mixture of Anglo-American, Hispanic, and Chinese. Since prejudice existed against the Chinese and Hispanics, they gravitated toward their own neighborhoods on the south and east ends of town, otherwise known as East Benson or the Lowlands or El Viejo. One example of prejudice was reflected in the wages paid to Chinese and Hispanic railroad workers or miners. They received substantially less compensation than their white counterparts. That discrepancy in wages caused huge problems in some neighboring towns like Bisbee.

Houses on the north side of the tracks where railroad workers usually lived were small in comparison to those on the south side.

Benson's population that first year hovered around 300, predominantly male, with all those railroad workers, miners, and cowboys. As the population grew through the decade, it continued to be mainly male. A man gets mighty thirsty after a hard day's labor. He needs a cool drink and a little entertainment, which explains the popularity and existence of so many saloons. Entertainment in a saloon centered around gambling, commonly a game of cards or roulette. Gambling in those days was not illegal and was an accepted activity among men. The combination of liquor, cheating, and sore losers, however, led to many a fistfight or gunplay. But the liquor and gambling weren't always enough for a lonely, single man wanting female companionship in a predominantly male population. And so came one more business in addition to the saloons.

Although prostitution was not exactly legal in early Arizona, laws against it were generally not enforced either. "Madams were often fined to keep the respectable citizens of the towns happy, but the amounts were usually small and the more often than not, the city officials were regular customers. The fact is that prostitutes in the Old West were good for the economy of a town and brought in money. So while respectable women crossed the street and refused to acknowledge the prostitutes, they were helping to add to a town's coffers and attracting new inhabitants to the area."[4] In Tombstone, no one bothered the girls as long as they bought a business license.

In mining and railroad towns, the brothel operated as a place of entertainment. The brothel in Benson on the southeast side of town near Gila and Second Street functioned the same way. It offered a dance hall, gambling tables, and a bar as well as the services of young women. "This bawdyhouse was the swingingest place in town. The tinny clinking of the piano, high-pitched laughter interspersed with loud hoot and hollers let the folks on main street know that business was open for another day. Although the house was some distance from downtown, voices and music carried easily to the merchants and patrons on the other side of the railroad tracks."[5]

"Benson as well as the miners' camps was in those early days rather 'wild and wooly.' There were saloons and gambling galore and the few people who lived 'in town' found it prudent to stay in their houses at night if they did not wish to take the chance of stopping stray bullets."[6] For example, Harry Blacklidge recalled a family story about his grandparents' arrival in Benson in 1880. Jacob and Lizzie Trask and their daughter Laura first stayed with their friends, the Kittridge family, until they could locate housing.

"The first afternoon, quite late near sundown, they heard shouting and shooting. Mama (daughter Laura Trask) ran to the front door and stepped outside. Almost at that same moment some 'characters' rode by shouting and firing their six-guns. Mrs. Kittridge grabbed mother and jerked her back inside where she gave the young lady quite a dressing down. Mother felt a jolt at her feet before Mrs. K grabbed her. The next morning they were out in front and found a bullet hole in the riser of the step mother was standing on."[7]

Some residents took extreme measures. "...during gunfights, (it is) rumored that Leonard Redfield, postmaster at the time, would put his wife inside the door of the safe to protect her from flying lead."[8]

Wild behavior in the streets was not uncommon in Benson's early days. After all, the Old Wild West thrived in the southern Arizona Territory during the 1880s. Fear of Indian attacks, shootouts, cowboys, saloons, hangings, fights: all the images one conjures up of the Wild West could be found in Benson. But that wasn't all. The quieter side of Benson—the families and shopkeepers, and the farmers and ranchers along the river—balanced the wilder side. Unlike the miners and cowboys and railroad workers who came for a job and would leave when it was finished, others came to stay. Early Benson would be struck time after time by tragedy. The pioneers who chose Benson as their home would build and rebuild, build and rebuild, as fires and floods ravaged the little town. They just didn't give up.

Chapter 2

The Mysterious Mr. Benson

Before the railroad traversed the southern Arizona Territory, hardy travelers crossed the San Pedro Valley in stagecoaches or in horse/mule/oxen-drawn wagons on a rough road just north of the future Benson. Settlers had already moved into the northern end of the valley, although not in great numbers. In St. David, established in 1877 on the east side of the San Pedro River, Mormon settlers farmed land close to the river. Farther north on the river, the agricultural community of Tres Alamos (*Three Cottonwoods*) had thrived for several decades.

Neither St. David nor Tres Alamos was established as a town or village but as a farming and ranching community. The two communities had small centers for a store or post office, school or church, but the majority of the community consisted of the farms and ranches that radiated outward in all directions. The center of Tres Alamos, for example, lay 10 miles north of the future Benson site on the east side of the river. Maps and charts showing Tres Alamos property owners include William Ohnesorgen, whose property lay a mile northeast of the future Benson in an area that would become Pomerene. Midway between the two farming communities of St. David and Tres Alamos, Peter Church and Jacob Horsch homesteaded land on the west side of the river. Church's and Horsch's properties would become Benson.

The Butterfield Overland Stage Company route once ran through Ohnesorgen's land where the company had built a stage station and a bridge for crossing the San Pedro River. After the company folded in 1861, travelers still used the road. Ownership of the stage station changed hands several times.

Jacob Schaublin and his wife kept the station until 1873. "If they had been paid according to the risks they have taken and the work they have done they would have been rich long ago. … Three soldiers are still left here as guard."[9] The "risks" and the need for soldiers reference the hostility of outlaws or Apaches who attacked stagecoaches and stage stations or raided the farms and ranches, usually for livestock. By December 1873, the partnership of Ohnesorgen and Eland operated the station. That partnership dissolved in February 1875, and William Ohnesorgen became the sole proprietor.

The station, described as an adobe building with 18" thick walls, offered a variety of services to travelers and locals: meals, beds, corrals, and a store featuring hay and grain. "The enterprising Mr. Ohnesorgen did a brisk business selling commodities to travelers and local inhabitants. In 1879, he erected a toll bridge over which mining supplies were transported to the new mining camps such as Fairbank and Tombstone. His stage depot marked the beginning of Benson as a link in the network of southwestern transportation."[10]

Built at a cost of $900, a costly project in 1879, Ohnesorgen's wood bridge replaced the original bridge built by Butterfield which had been washed out by a flood. The new toll bridge spanned 25 feet across the river and facilitated passage across it. When people complained about paying the toll, Ohnesorgen told them they were welcome to cross the river elsewhere without paying a toll. But, of course, he knew the difficulties of crossing the river, especially with heavy loads or when the river was swollen by rains.

"My! How the people hated to pay toll. They declared it was a public highway. I told them the highway went through the river and they could use it if they wished, but the bridge was on my land and if they used it, they would pay toll."[11]

The stage station operated under several names: Ohnesorgen Stage Station, San Pedro Crossing, or the Middle Crossing. An 1880 business directory for Arizona lists a Benson City, with a single entry under it: "Ohnesorgen Wm, stage station." Thus begins the quest to find out how Benson received its name.

Some believe that Ohnesorgen's station was associated with

Howard Walker and William (Billy) Ohnesorgan. Photo taken after the stage station closed and Ohnesorgan moved his business to Benson. Courtesy San Pedro Valley Arts & Historical Society.

the name Benson as a compliment to Henry McKinley Benson, an Army lieutenant stationed at various posts in Southern Arizona to protect settlers. "Since a schedule of stage stops, printed in 1880, lists 'Benson City, William Ohnesorgen, owner and keeper,' it would seem that Jesse Wien and (Senator) Carl Hayden have the best answer in believing that Benson was named for the Lieutenant."[12] Jesse Wien was an early Benson resident and the first town marshal. Senator Carl Hayden represented Arizona in the U.S. House of Representatives and U.S. Senate for a total of 56 years from 1912 to 1969. Their statements, however, are not documented.

Although the town of Benson did not physically exist until June of 1880, the site and name of the new town were known well before then. Because of the proximity of the stage station to the future town, it would be logical for Ohnesorgen, an astute businessman, to associate his stage station with the future town for name recognition. Ohnesorgen also ran a stage line by 1879 with partner Howard C. Walker between Ohnesorgen's Bridge, Tucson, and Tombstone. Listing the stage station's or stage line's location with a town name and railroad stop is more recognizable to travelers than just Ohnesorgen's Bridge. A listing under Benson also helped to distinguish it from the stage station and crossing at Tres Alamos. By 1881, the "City" is dropped in directories, and the town was listed simply as "Benson."

A biography of Lieutenant Henry McKinley Benson in the Arizona State University library also attributes the source of Benson's name to the lieutenant. "The railroad station and town of Benson, Cochise County, Arizona, was named for him."[13] The biography, however, is a typewritten manuscript without author, date, sources, or other bibliographic information.

Years before the railroad arrived, federal surveyors had

plotted the best course for a railroad and the best place to cross the river. In a manuscript, Clara C. Colvin said the town was named after a Major Benson, who she claims made one of the first railroad surveys through the area. However, she is the only person to nominate the major and does not offer any documentation to support her theory.

Before Charles Crocker, president of Southern Pacific Railroad, constructed a railway station, and thereby a town, he needed land. To get the land he needed, Crocker used the Pacific Improvement Company, a land holding company, which he and his partners had recently started. The company bought Peter Church's and Jacob Horsch's homesteads. Together their homesteads totaled 160 acres. The Pacific Improvement Company paid each homesteader $400 for his land, which was at least double what the government charged for buying non-homesteaded land. The company platted an entire town on those 160 acres, dividing the land into blocks and then subdividing the blocks into lots. The plat map for Benson was completed by April 1880, three months before the railroad tracks reached the Benson site on June 14th. When Pacific Improvement offered the lots for sale a week later on June 21st

for $177 per lot, it only had to sell five lots to cover the cost of buying the homesteads to make a profit. The company easily accomplished that the first day the lots were offered for sale.

Map coordinates for the Church's and Horsch's homesteads listed in the Bureau of Land Management records match the map coordinates for the city of Benson in the Cochise County Recorder's Office, except for a few acres in northeast Benson. The company bought the extra acreage, identified as being non-homesteaded land in Tres Alamos, for $10 from George Hill Howard. A lawsuit ensued because Howard didn't have clear title to the land, but the courts upheld the purchase by Pacific Improvement.

With the railroad came those offering services to the workers, such as Chinese who cooked or did their laundry. Others just followed the railroad into new territory. In a newspaper article, "Telling It Like It Was..." Clara Eder refers to the speculation that 'Benson' comes from the name of "a peddler known to have followed the railroad construction crew."[14] The 1935 edition of *Arizona Name Places* also refers to the peddler and quotes a letter written by Leonard Redfield, long-time Benson postmaster, who said that "Benson was named by the S.P.R.R. (Southern Pacific Railroad) for a peddler who made frequent trips through this place in the early days."

The 1960 edition of *Arizona Name Places* revised by Bryd Granger, however, cites a different origin for Benson's name without any explanation or citation as to why he made the change. Granger later wrote *Arizona Names: X Marks the Spot* and uses the same information as his revised edition of *Arizona Name Places*. Both reference books say that Charles Crocker, president of the Southern Pacific Railroad, named the town after his friend Judge William B. Benson.

The question of Judge Benson's full name is an excellent

example of how accurate or inaccurate one can be writing about history without documented sources. Although William B. is the most common, other sources than those cited above say the judge's first name and middle initial were William A. or William S. So is William's middle initial A, B, or S? None of the sources cite an original source for their choice.

To further confuse the issue, the April 1, 1880 edition of the *Arizona Weekly Star* newspaper in Tucson reported, "Benson is to be the name of the railroad city of the San Pedro, which has already been located and will probably be the point from which the Tombstone and southeastern freight will be delivered. The name is in honor of John Benson of San Francisco, who was one of Charles Crocker's guests during his late visit to our city. We hope for the sake of its Godfather that Benson city may be a bright and shining light in the galaxy of cities which are now springing up in the silvery clime of Arizona." Crocker seems to have four friends with the last name of Benson: William A., William B., William S., and John. At least for John documentation exists for Benson being his namesake, a record written during the period when Benson was named. The assumption here is that the newspaper was accurate in reporting Benson's first name.

The *Arizona Weekly Star* article is dated April 1, 1880, months before the railroad reached the location for Benson. The date does coincide with the completion of the plat map for Benson. The April 30, 1880 edition of the *Weekly Arizona Miner*, a Prescott newspaper, also reveals the name of the new town as Benson. So the name of the town was known and publicized before the town existed. This may explain why Ohnesorgen knew in advance to list his stage station under the name "Benson City" in the business directory. As a local, he would also have been aware of the sale of his neighbors' homesteads before any public announcements. The publicity before the founding of the town also eliminates the theory of the town being named after a peddler who in one case followed the construction crew into town and in the other, "made frequent trips through this place in the early days." The name Benson predates any visits by the peddler.

A peddler or a major, a lieutenant or a judge, or just a friend: all contending for the honor of having a town named after them. Lots of theories offered; little proof provided. A definitive answer as to the origin of Benson's name has most likely been lost in the pages of history. Perhaps one day, somebody will turn one of those pages, and there the answer will be.

Chapter 3

Benson's Neighbors

To understand Benson's growth and importance in the San Pedro Valley, it is necessary to take a peek at what was happening elsewhere in the valley. Development was not a tidy progression; it was more like an explosion of activity with many things happening at the same time. Benson and neighboring towns to the south not only grew up together, but their dependence on each other intertwined their fates.

The enduring towns of Tombstone, St. David, and Fort Huachuca began only a few years earlier than Benson in 1877; the same year the railroad started its trek across the desert from Yuma. Bisbee began the same year as Benson in 1880. The story of the development of the valley, however, predates any of these towns; it begins with the Indians.

The San Pedro Valley has a long history of occupancy from the pre-historic Clovis people to various Native American cultures who called it home. No Native American group would match the power and dominance of the Chiricahua Apaches. They controlled most of what would become Cochise County and parts of northern Mexico. The arrival of the Spanish in the valley strengthened that dominance.

The Spanish knew of the existence of the San Pedro Valley

for centuries. As early as 1540, Francisco Coronado used the valley corridor as a passage on his journey north in his search for the Seven Cities of Gold. Coronado encountered the Chiricahua Apaches on his journey. Serious attempts at settlement along the San Pedro River did not begin until the late 17th century when Father Eusebio Francisco Kino founded the Quiburi Mission in 1692 and settlers established "rancheros" along the river a few years later. However, continuous raids by the Chiricahua Apaches posed too much of a risk and thwarted settlement. Even the building of presidios with their military forces in the late 1700s could not curb the ever-looming danger from the Apaches.

Inadvertently, the Spanish had helped the Apaches by introducing them to the horse. The Apaches recognized their value and adopted them into their culture. The horse allowed the Apaches greater freedom of movement for hunting, gathering, raiding, or moving among their seasonal campsites. With this increased mobility, the Apaches dominated the valley. They "… raided Spanish mines, settlements, and ranches farther south in Sonora and prevented non-Indian settlement in the San Pedro watershed for more than 100 years."[15]

When Mormons settlers arrived and founded St. David in 1877, they began farming on the fertile banks of the San Pedro River. Tres Alamos, another small farming community, lay several miles to the north. For both communities, it was a risky time. Apaches raided their farms, driving off horses predominantly, but also oxen and mules. They broke into houses and destroyed property and sometimes killed the farmers or their families. With the outside threat from the Apaches, Anglos and Hispanics in Tres Alamos bonded together against a common threat and little prejudice existed between the two ethnic groups.

Benson's Ride through History: 1880 - 1945

San Pedro Valley circa 1880s

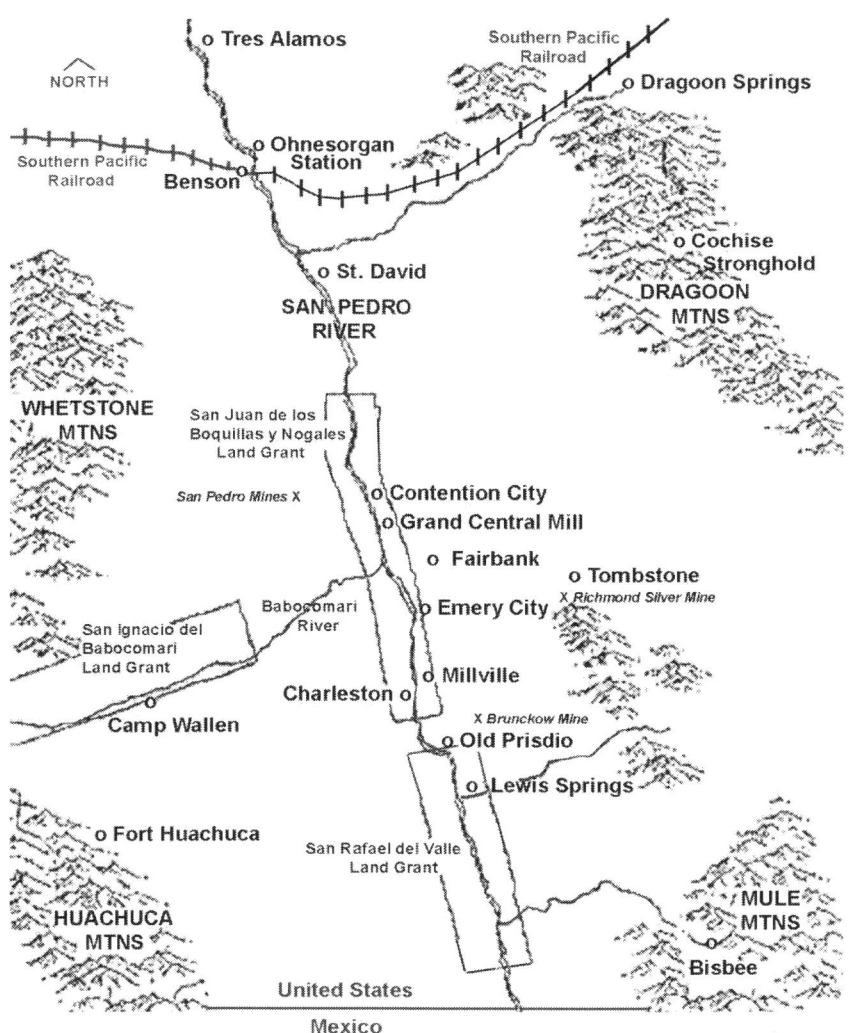

This illustration portrays the relative position of some of the major landmarks in the valley. It is not a complete representation of all the towns, mines, and ranches in the valley.

In their efforts to keep the 'white man' out of the valley, the Apaches unintentionally contributed to their own downfall. Their hostile activity brought the soldiers and scouts. Various army posts existed in different locations, but none endured until Captain Samuel Whitside selected the slopes of the Huachuca Mountains as the site for his post in 1877. The site offered many advantages for the soldiers: "... fresh running water, an abundance of trees, excellent observation in three directions, and protective high ground against Apache tactical methods. ... [Its location also] blocked traditional Apache escape routes to Mexico."[16]

The existence of the camp helped protect civilians and travel routes. "Apache unrest had deterred prospectors from exploring what is now Cochise County. However, the establishment of Camp Huachuca in the Huachuca Mountains in February of 1877 brought a measure of security to the region, and set the stage for the discovery of the Tombstone mines."[17]

From Camp Huachuca, soldiers pursued the Apaches across southern Arizona. They communicated via a heliograph, a signaling device that used a moveable mirror to reflect beams of light. The Army maintained several heliograph stations, one of them on Signal Hill near Benson. Camp Huachuca became Fort Huachuca in 1882.

Threat of menace from the Apaches also played a role in the first six years of Benson's growth. The Apaches never raided Benson, but they reportedly killed three men in different locations on the outskirts of town. Residents lived under constant fear. When sisters Dolores and Francisca Celaya planned their double wedding for February 3, 1883, they had a problem. There was no Catholic church in Benson. To be married in the church meant traveling to Tombstone. To transport brides, grooms Francisco Gauna and Genaro Lopez

Figueroa respectively, parents, and attendants required two covered wagons. "It took them three days to travel from Benson to Tombstone as they had to travel mostly by night to avoid meeting with Indians who were very wild in those days."[18] Indians feared the dark and did not travel at night. Fortunately, all went well for the marriage ceremony. Francisca had married at age 13 and bore 15 children, nine of whom died in infancy.

Harry J. Blacklidge related a family story about an encounter typifying the ominous atmosphere the Apaches created. When Jacob Trask moved his family to Benson in 1880, they squatted on property about five miles south of Benson on the road to Tombstone. For a living, Jacob drove his ten-mule team back and forth to Tombstone delivering supplies. He refused to carry a rifle for protection against Apaches. "What's the use, they'd see me first and kill me before I got a chance to use it."[19] The job kept him away from home two days at a time, leaving his wife and children alone on the somewhat secluded property: a perfect target for Apaches who preferred assaulting isolated individuals or small groups.

"One night," Blacklidge said, "while he (Jacob) was away and they were getting ready for bed, Grandma happened to look out the back window and, in the bright moonlight, saw Indians at the well. Scared stiff. But after a while they (family) blew the light out and grabbed up a few trinkets, including a new pair of shoes that Grandma had gotten the last trip to town, and sneaked out the front door and headed for the road some three hundred yards away, where the Tombstone stage was due to pass within a half hour. They made the stage okay. Next morning a posse of citizens headed out before daylight. They returned in a couple of hours. Turned out they were friendly Papago Indians traveling through, selling baskets and ollas. The payoff came when they returned to the ranch and Grandma remembered she had left three hundred dollars in gold wrapped in a piece of paper and stuck up over one of the rafters."[20]

Apache activity around Benson did not include attacking the railroad. They did not attempt to interfere with its building across the eastern Arizona Territory. "Apaches maintained a respectful distance from the trains, but lonely trackwalkers (railway inspectors) were among their victims."[21]

Geronimo, the most notorious of the Chiricahua Apaches, surrendered with his band of warriors in 1886, ending the threat of Apache attacks. The Apaches were removed from the area and sent to Florida. They left Bowie station on September 6, 1886, never to return as a

Geronimo (above) and his wife Ta-ayz-slath and a son (right). Courtesy Wikimedia.

tribe to their lands in the Chiricahua Mountains. After Geronimo's surrender, the soldiers from Fort Huachuca turned their attention to guarding the U.S. border where trouble still brewed from renegade Indians, Mexican bandits, and American outlaws.

Soldiers and scouts not only pursued Apaches to protect

settlers, but their forays into the hills and mountains led to the discovery of mineral ores and the founding of Tombstone and Bisbee, as well as numerous smaller towns and mines all around the area. A frenzy of prospecting throughout the West had begun in 1848 with the discovery of gold in California. Fear of the Apaches kept the prospectors at bay in the San Pedro Valley until the presence of soldiers offered a measure of safety in the area. The mining industry was about to explode in the region.

Towns sprang up overnight at the news of a strike; many died just as quickly. Mining towns often began as 'tent cities.' Tents were later replaced by small frame 'moveable' houses without foundations. They were built in sections, so they could be assembled and disassembled when their owners heard of a new strike and moved to the next location. They simply took their houses with them because building materials were not easily accessible in the Southwest desert.

The first big mining boom came when Edward Lawrence Schieffelin discovered silver in the hills east of Camp Huachuca, an area that lay in the heart of Apache country. Knowing the danger of entering territory not many miles from Cochise's Stronghold, an Apache camp, he decided to follow a scouting party from the camp, thinking they would afford him some measure of protection. But he soon discovered that keeping up with the scouting party left him no time to prospect, so he struck out on his own. When he returned to the camp to restock his supplies, the soldiers asked if he had found anything. "Several times, in reply to my remark that I would eventually find something in that country, the soldiers said, 'Yes, you'll find your tombstone'." [22]

After Schieffelin filed his claim on August 1, 1877, he brought in his brother Albert and assayer Richard Gird. Other miners quickly flocked to the area and filed numerous claims for their share of the wealth. The mining camp of Tombstone became a boomtown, the largest in the Arizona Territory. In the early 1880s, the population in Benson is estimated at 300, in Tombstone 15,000. Because of its size, when the Arizona legislature established Cochise County on February 1, 1881, it named Tombstone as the first county seat. When Tombstone's fate shifted, the county seat moved to Bisbee in 1929.

In terms of production, Tombstone did not fare as well as Bisbee. It started to decline in the mid-1880s when the silver mines penetrated the water table and water flooded the mines. "Attempts to pump out the water marginally worked for a few years but soon became too costly to continue."[23] Combined with a drop in the price of silver, labor problems, and even Tombstone's reputation for shootings and violence, mining operations never fully recovered. The closure of mines may well have turned Tombstone into a ghost town. But the very reputation that adversely affected it during its early years helped to keep it alive. The town thrives as a tourist attraction because of its notoriety as "the town too tough to die."

Tombstone's decline adversely affected many of the smaller towns near it. "During the 1880s, Charleston, Millville, Emory City, and Contention City were short-lived mill towns on the San Pedro River that processed ore from the Tombstone mines. Ore milling required an abundant supply of water, so the mill towns had to be near the river. By 1886, most of these towns were abandoned and milling was done in Tombstone, using surplus water pumped out of the mines."[24] The mill towns became ghost towns.

Another ghost town, Fairbank, originally gained its importance as a railroad supply and stage depot for Tombstone. In the early days of Tombstone's boom, three stage companies ran lines to serve Benson, Tombstone, and Tucson. They were owned by Wells Fargo, by J.D. Kinnear, and by Billy Ohnesorgen and Howard C. Walker. Ohnesorgen and Walker started their stage line in 1879 as the Tucson and Tombstone Stage Line but later renamed it the Ohnesorgen & Walker Stage Co. Fierce competition led to a price war. While Ohnesorgen and Walker posted rates for the trip between Tucson and Tombstone at $7.00, Kinnear undercut them at $4.00. Ohnesorgen, a highly respected Benson resident, had to mortgage his ranch to cover losses and eventually dropped out of the business by selling his share to Walker. Kinnear and Walker later merged as the railroad cut into their business. Numerous stage robberies occurred along the routes of all of the stage lines, some resulting in injury or death.

When the New Mexico & Arizona Railroad completed a line from Fairbank to Benson in 1882, it shortened the time and distance it took to reach the Southern Pacific from Tombstone by stage or freight wagon. Supplies or passengers could travel by rail from Benson to Fairbank and then transfer to a stage line, or vice versa, rather than making the full 25 mile trip to and from Benson by stage.

In later years, railroad tracks ran directly into Tombstone, Bisbee, and beyond, making a stop in Fairbank unnecessary. The town survived for several decades because the Boquillas Land and Cattle Company purchased all the land in town in 1901 and used Fairbank as its headquarters and cattle shipping station. With the breakup of large cattle ranches like Boquillas, the town once again lost its function. "The town still had people living there well into the 1950s, but the town was slowly dying and by the 1970s only a roadside store with a gas pump remained. By the mid-1970s, the last few of its residents closed the store and moved away."[25]

Before the decline of Tombstone and the mill towns,

however, another foray into the hills resulted in a find even bigger than the Tombstone mines. While searching for water in the Mule Mountains, a detail of soldiers from Fort Bowie found evidence of mineral deposits that would lead to the discovery of a variety of ores, including gold and silver, but mostly copper. In Bisbee, copper was queen.

The rush began after Jack Dunn, a civilian scout stationed at Fort Bowie, filed the first claim. Prospectors flocked to the area; tents and shacks popped up everywhere. Bisbee was born. "By August 1880 miners had filed claims on more than 200 mine locations, and enough people had arrived to justify town amenities such as a school and sheriff."[26] By winter, the Copper Queen Company employed over 100 miners. The Queen Mine, absorbed by Phelps-Dodge in 1884, would thrive for the next century; the copper ore extracted from the mines valued in the billions. "Activities began to slow as the mines played out and the population began to shrink; mining operations on a large scale became unprofitable in 1975."[27] By that time, however, the picturesque town nestled on the hillsides had developed enough other businesses to sustain it.

As the fate of all these towns was intertwined, the decline of the mines threatened Benson's survival too.

Chapter 4

Bad Boys

Wild behavior in the streets was not uncommon in Benson's early days. After all, the Old West thrived in the southeastern Arizona Territory during the late 1880s and early 1900s due to the combination of rough living conditions, a lack of sufficient number of law enforcers, and the temporary status of most town dwellers. Benson's population its first year hovered around 300 comprised mostly of railroad workers, miners, and cowboys. It was a predominantly male and transient population. As the population grew through the decade, it continued to be primarily male. In four years, the population of Benson doubled; in thirty years, it quadrupled.

That the population was transient is important. Transients were not interested in the growth of a town or in settling down or in becoming law-abiding citizens. They came temporarily for an opportunity and would move on. In the meanwhile, they'd just whoop it up and have a good time. Their behavior gave rise to the reputation of the Wild West.

Despite efforts to establish law and order, lawlessness ruled during Benson's earliest years. Historian Edward Ellsworth compiled Corner Inquest Reports from 1881 to 1889 for people buried in the Seventh Street Cemetery. Of those he found, shootings account for 63% of the deaths. Only half of those identify the shooter. Not all of these records deal with unlawful activity. Railroad accidents caused a number of deaths. Rafaela Disonra died of "excessive" old age. He was 80.

But not one of the inquest reports mention hanging. Death by hanging was the Old West's answer to swift 'justice,' often carried out by vigilantes: citizens who sometimes reacted in the heat of the moment more from tempers, liquor, or prejudice than from investigation of the facts. Otherwise stable, law-abiding citizens simply "had enough" and took the law into their own hands to rid the town of undesirables. In such cases, once done, it was not talked about and no records existed of the execution.

In August of 1881, a gunfight erupted in Benson involving the Top and Bottom Gang. So notorious was their reputation as thieves and highwaymen that the *Arizona Weekly Citizen* commented, "Better the unfortunate victims of these men be in the hands of the Apaches than in the clutches of this gang."[28] A dispute over a game of cards initially led to a fistfight between Ed Byrnes and Mart (Chuck) Maloney. But on day two of the disagreement, they brought out the pistols.

Byrnes and Maloney fired at each other and missed. One of Byrnes' bullets, however, accidently hit Deputy Sheriff Hiram McComus as he approached the two to stop the gunplay. The bullet hit McComus in the leg and he fell to the ground. Several citizens carried the deputy into a nearby house, then chased down Byrnes yelling about a lynching. "There was a rumor last evening that Byrnes, of the top and bottom game notoriety, had been lynched at Benson, but the news was too good to be true."[29]

Deputy Sheriff William Breckenridge of Tombstone happened to be in Benson when Byrnes shot McComus. He arrested the gunman and took him into custody. Byrnes was charged with "assault to commit murder on Deputy Sheriff McComus," but was later "discharged from custody"[30] after examination by a Court Commissioner.

Byrnes' arrest did not appease the townsfolk. Immediately after his arrest, they took all the furniture out of the saloon the gang frequented and burned it in the street. "The gang was invited to leave town before sundown and promised a necktie party in their honor if they remained. The outlaws took a train for Tucson that evening."[31] The Top and Bottom Gang got off with a warning. Not all outlaws, or suspected outlaws, were so lucky.

Some people believe myths and repeat them as fact. Such is the case when someone claims that large paddleboats or steamboats used to navigate the San Pedro River. The Colorado River, perhaps; the San Pedro, no. The San Pedro is not and never was wide enough nor deep enough for a paddleboat. On the other hand, generations of Bensonites treated the story of Los Triaditos, *the castoffs*, as merely a myth. It isn't.

Three Mexicans were buried beneath a mesquite tree in unmarked graves outside the cemetery. Courtesy Edward Ellsworth.

Again in the early 1880s, probably 1882 or 1883, three Mexicans, Los Triaditos, met their end in a lumber yard without benefit of trial, without any record of their names or their deaths. Had it not been for the Mexican community, the victims would have faded into oblivion. Two of the Mexicans were accused of attempting a train robbery, the third of horse-stealing. Since local mesquite trees are too short and flexible for hangings, vigilantes marched them to the local lumber yard and hanged them from a crossbeam. Once the noose had completed its work, their bodies were taken off the gallows and put into wood coffins. Locals refused to allow their burial in the cemetery, considered to be hallowed ground and not fitting for outlaws. Instead, they were buried outside the south end of the cemetery, across an arroyo under a mesquite tree. Two wood crosses marked their graves for many years.

The Mexican Catholic community believed their souls went to limbo, a place between Heaven and Hell for the lost or forgotten. Only by helping those still on earth could these souls redeem themselves and enter Heaven. And so the community began visiting their graves, tending to them, and leaving candles as a symbol of their prayers and wishes. As late as World War I, candles flickered through the night, candle drippings adorned the tree branches, and broken shards of candle holders littered the ground.

Years passed and the tradition faded. The wood crosses rotted and disappeared. The Mexican community no longer visited the graves. No more candles flickered in the night. People forgot. Local historians questioned whether or not there was any truth to the story. Elizabeth Brenner, representative of Benson's Historical Preservation Commission, her husband Don, and historians Edward Ellsworth and Vay Fenn decided to find out.

Unearthing the bones of Los Triaditos buried 8 ft. deep. Courtesy Edward Ellsworth.

On April 4 and 5, 2008, they went to the burial site and Vay Fenn began excavating with his backhoe. At six feet, finding nothing, they began to despair. However, knowing that fill had been added to the arroyo over the years, they kept digging. Eight feet down, they found bones.

The wood coffins had long since deteriorated, but the nails that once held them together remained. Two of the bodies had been buried head to foot in one coffin; the third body, with its head missing, in another. Carefully, the historians collected the bones and put them into three plastic containers. They then dug a grave for each man inside the south wall of the 7th

New graves for Los Triaditos inside the cemetery. Courtesy Edward Ellsworth.

St. Cemetery, just across the arroyo from their original burial site, and re-interred the bones. History has hidden the men's names, their guilt or innocence shall never be proved or disproved, but at least after more than 125 years, their new, marked graves in the cemetery attest to their existence and violent deaths.

"Back in 1887, Benson was still a raw western town and law was carried in a man's pocket."[32] Typical of the Old Wild West and a transient male population which had little respect for the law, arguments were settled with guns. One responded to threats with a gun. Sometimes gunplay erupted when the boys were just whooping it up and having fun. The editor of the *Tombstone Epitaph* in covering news about Benson in 1882 said, "Last evening some of the 'boys' got to shooting at the 'stars,' but as I am not in communication with those planets I can't say whether or not anybody up there was killed."[33]

In March 1906, Harry Fisher "while on a spree shot up the town of Benson and was compelled by Justice Titus to contribute the sum of $100 to the county treasury."[34] One of his bullets went through a window in the Southern Pacific Depot hitting a lamp on one of the tables, narrowly missing a clerk at work in the office. "... the few people who lived 'in town' found it prudent to stay in their houses at night if they did not wish to take the chance of stopping stray bullets."[35] Out on the range, justice was also meted out with a gun. For rustlers, according to rancher Gerry McGoffin, "They'd just be shot. There wouldn't be a trial or anything. They'd just be shot."[36]

The slightest displeasure could trigger gun use, as in the case of Charlie Henderson (or Henricksen, depending on the source). Railroads often shared their water supply with residents of small towns, whether from a cistern, a tank car, or a well. In Benson's case, it was a well. Southern Pacific had dug a deep well to provide water for their train locomotives. Residents who had not dug their own wells went to the pump house for buckets of water for domestic use.

Charlie Henderson was in charge of the pump house in Benson. He particularly liked the pretty Mexican ladies who came for buckets of water and charged each of them a kiss as payment for the water. No kiss, no water. The ladies may not have been as happy with the arrangement as Charlie was. In April 1884, Ciprano Cruz went to the pump house himself. "Charlie saw his cozy arrangement threatened and refused to serve the man. Cruz tried to take the water, but Henderson became irate and shot and killed him."[37] Henderson was arrested.

This case has been cited as an example of the racial prejudice that existed in early Benson. While Anglos and Hispanics united in Tres Alamos against their common enemy, the Apaches, the development of an Anglo town offered no such unifying factor. It is doubtful Charlie would ever have demanded a kiss from white women coming to the pump house. The community or Southern Pacific would have stopped him. He felt safe, however, in extorting sexual favors from Hispanic women.

The railroad had troubles of its own. One night in 1881, a Wells, Fargo & Co. stage carrying bars of silver bullion drove up to the depot platform to unload. "While the messenger was taking them into the building, necessitating his absence from the platform only for a few seconds at a time, some person or persons got away with one of the bars, valued in the neighborhood of $2,000. Diligent search was immediately made and Wells, Fargo & Co. offered a reward of $450 for the recovery of the bullion and $300 each for the parties implicated in any way to the theft."[38] No clue was found to identify the daring robbers.

Another incident took place at the Benson railroad yard in 1882 which prompted the *Tombstone Epitaph* to say: "The industrious scoundrels, who are rapidly earning an unenviable reputation for the town of Benson, added another to their long list of outrages and crimes."[39] Railroad workers left two passenger cars on the track a couple of hundred feet back from the station while the railroad switched cars. Busy at their tasks, the workers were unaware that robbers had entered an unguarded car. "Four of the scoundrels stood at each of the four doors and with pistols in hand commanded silence. The rest of the robbers then ransacked the two cars and took everything of value that could be found, even going as far as taking gold rings and jewelry from women and young girls. One old woman who was traveling to California with her two daughters had a purse containing $270 forcefully taken from her clinched hand; an old man had a pair of fine boots taken off his feet, and three young girls who were sleeping in a corner of one of the cars were robbed of their bedding. It took about fifteen minutes to complete the job, and the robbers absconded and have not been heard of since."[40]

It is interesting that the reporter who wrote about the above incident spoke of Benson "rapidly earning an unenviable reputation." It's questionable that Benson with its population of 300 could compete with Tombstone for the title of Wildest Town in the West, although some claim it to be true. "By 1881 Tombstone's population had increased to around 4,000 – 5,000. Legend has it that this figure counted only the white male registered voters that were over 21 years of age and if you take into account the women, children, Chinese, Mexicans and the many 'ladies of the evening' they say the population was between 15,000 and 20,000 people. It is more likely that the population was closer to 7,000- 9,000."[41]

In the early 1880s, 92 saloons lined Allen Street, the main street in Tombstone. Benson had eight, not including the bars in hotels. The Bird Cage Theatre in Tombstone, perched at the east end of Allen Street, offered a man all types of pleasures as a saloon, theatre, gambling hall, and brothel. And the pleasures went on day or night, seven days a week, until it closed in 1889. While Benson had its house of ill-repute, it never earned a reputation as the "… wildest, wickedest night spot between Basin Street and the Barbary Coast" as the Bird Cage did from the New York Times. Nor did it have an alleged 140 bullet holes found in the walls and ceiling.

During its heyday, Tombstone had earned a bad reputation for too much gun play and too many shootings. But no shootout has even matched the saga of what happened on October 26, 1881 at the O.K. Corral between the Earps and the Cowboys. Those 30 shots in 24 seconds have generated almost a century and a half of discussion and controversy.

Benson's most famous shootout occurred on Thanksgiving Day in 1906. The Fashion Saloon, formerly the Wildcat Saloon, was crowded. According to the customers, proprietor Harry K. Fisher had been quarreling with his bartender Jack McCullough all evening. As midnight approached, "… before anyone realized what was going on each of the parties to the dispute had whipped out a gun and started shooting."[42]

McCullough, using an old style Colt revolver, quickly fired three shots. One shot hit Fisher in the hip. Fisher, using the new Colt automatic, fired six shots. All six hit the bartender. Witnesses said McCullough fired first and Fisher returned fire only after McCullough had shot at him several times.

When the shooting stopped, the crowd scattered to find a physician and an officer. Ranger Lieutenant Harry Wheeler happened to be close to the saloon and heard the shots. He arrived as the crowd dispersed. Wheeler arrested Fisher, who turned over his gun without any resistance. A physician arrived, pronounced McCullough dead, and tended to Fisher's wound.

Fisher was held without bail until the district attorney conducted a preliminary examination of the case on December 8th. Public opinion favored Fisher. "It is the consensus of opinion that he will be restored to liberty on the ground that he had to shoot to protect his life."[43] But he wasn't freed at the preliminary hearing. Fisher was later granted bail in the amount of $2,500. By December 13th, Fisher still sat in jail awaiting delivery of his bail to the clerk's office in Tombstone. He also waited for the grand jury to convene and decide what, if any, charges he might face for killing McCullough. Unfortunately, the newspapers did not cover the outcome.

This story is Benson's most famous shootout because of the stories written about it in future years. It is also a good example of the difficulties in writing a history. Information for the version of the story given above is taken from newspaper articles written at the time of the incident. Newspapers are considered a fairly reliable source. However, even newspapers with a good reputation for factual reporting have reporters who embellish stories and/or do not get their facts straight. A case in point: In the coverage of this shooting, some articles from the *Bisbee Daily Review* gives the bartender's name as P. McCollum. Other articles in the same newspaper, however, use the name Jack McCullough. McCollum had a bad reputation and a nickname of Jack the Ripper which may be why he was referred to as Jack McCollum.

Testimony by eye-witnesses is not always reliable either: ask any policeman who hears varying versions of the same event. A dramatic incident appeals to writers of historical events who years later take the basic facts and add details or

Benson's Ride through History: 1880 - 1945

conclusions to make a story more colorful. Were those added details the result of research or did the writer fictionalize the story? Based on numerous retellings about this shooting, a more colorful version goes something like this:

Benson's most famous shootout occurred on Thanksgiving Day in 1906. Train after train brought passengers to town. Many of these passengers were bound for points south, but a strike in Sonora stranded all Mexico-bound trains. With nothing else to do, and with the Fashion Saloon conveniently located just across the street from the depot, the male passengers headed for the saloon.

The saloon offered not only drinking, but gambling at the roulette wheel and card tables, a pot-bellied stove for warmth, saloon girls for entertainment, and someone occasionally banging out a tune on the old piano. If the scene sounds like the perfect setting for a western movie, it was, only it was real, and the drinking, gambling, and tempers would lead to the most infamous shootout in Benson's history.

Jack the Ripper worked for Harry Fisher, owner of the Fashion Saloon. 'Twas a strange handle Jack had chosen for himself, but in those days, no one questioned why, or knew his real name. His experience as a bartender, roulette croupier, and card dealer was all Harry needed to know. That Thanksgiving morning, Jack worked the roulette wheel, and by 1:00 p.m. when they closed the saloon for a few hours to eat their holiday dinner, Harry counted roulette profits of $612, the equivalent of over $16,000 in 2020. Harry pocketed $600, and handed Jack $12 as a tip, a tip of approximately two percent. Jack was not pleased with such a small tip and said so. But he shrugged it off, and as the two left to go eat, they chatted amiably. The slight had not yet had time to fester.

When the bar reopened, the crowd swelled as the cowboys

arrived to join the festivities. Jack tended bar during the evening and apparently served himself, as well as the customers, more than a few drinks. As the hours wore on, customers heard him grumbling about Harry's stinginess. Finally, the rowdiness and booze brought Jack's feelings to a boil.

Jack grabbed his gun and shot out the large ceiling lamp, leaving the bar in semi-darkness. His next shot knocked out the small lamp on the piano. In the darkness, customers scrambled for the door or sought cover. A third shot produced a cry of pain, then a responding volley of bullets.

Silence. The crowd began to edge its way back to the doorway. In the dim light, they saw Jack leaning on the bar. He slowly began to tip backwards, then fell to the floor. Harry, clutching his buttocks, appeared in the doorway yelling for the doctor.

As Dr. Charles Powell attended to Fisher, he explained to Arizona Ranger Harry Wheeler that when Jack's third shot hit him, he responded in kind to protect his customers. The on-the-spot inquest cleared Jessie of any wrong-doing. The next day while Jack the Ripper was quietly buried, it was business as usual, except, of course, for the new bartender.

An earlier saloon shooting on May 2, 1902, did not receive the same notoriety. James Shepard and Charles Livingston both worked at the Land Saloon, later renamed the Turf, but they did not get along. Shepard tended bar all night on May 1st, but instead of going to bed after his shift, he "proceeded during the day to load himself with booze."[44] The liquor and lack of sleep finally took its toll, and Shepard fell asleep at the roulette table. Charles Morath picked Shepard up and took him to a bed in a back room where Livingston had been lying. Livingston got up and tried to help Morath put Shepard into the bed.

Only Shepard didn't want to go to bed and resisted.

According to Morath, during their struggle with Shepard, Livingston's hand slipped, scratching Shepard's face and drawing a little blood. Livingston and Morath left Shepard in the room, but he didn't stay there for long. Livingston went to the bar, and while the bartender fetched him a bottle of beer, Shepard came out of the back room, walked behind the bar, and picked up the bar's revolver. He stood just opposite Livingston on the other side of bar and fired one fatal shot. Shepard was arrested and charged with murder.

"Those who witnessed the killing and who knew Shepard, say that there was never a more cold-blooded murder ... they believe Shepard knew precisely what he was going to do."[45] And the coroner's jury determined that Livingston "died from a gunshot wound inflicted by one James Shepard. We further find that the shooting which caused this death was premeditated and unjustifiable."[46]

During the trial, Shepard accused Livingston of having beaten him up in the back room and that he acted in self-defense because he was fearful for his life. Shepard's first trial ended in a hung jury. His second trial ended in December 1903 with a "not guilty" verdict.

Westerns popularized many images of the Old West, the inside of the Fashion Saloon being one. Another well-known scene places the sheriff on the main street in town, his gun loaded and ready at his side, challenging the lawbreaker while folks watch from the sidewalks. Just a few months after the demise of Jack the Ripper, such a gunfight erupted on the streets of Benson on February 28, 1907. It started out in the stereotypic way, but ended with a twist that made it one of the most unusual gunfights in the annals of the West.

The story actually began in late 1905 when an unnamed brunette in her mid-twenties, tall and shapely, met D.W.

Silverton in Nevada. She also met another man in Nevada, J.A. Tracy, shortly thereafter in early 1906. A year later, 1907, Tracy was working at Vail Station as an agent for the Helvetia Copper Company. The brunette was in Tucson with Silverton. According to one version of the story, Mr. and Mrs. Silverton claimed to be married by an itinerant preacher, but had no license.

When Tracy heard that she was in Tucson, he went to see her. "... he paid her a visit to offer her a diamond ring. She declined, and Tracy returned to Vail's Station without comment. The next day, however, she received four threatening letters from her frustrated suitor."[47]

Meanwhile, the Silvertons decided to take the train to tour Douglas, Bisbee, and Cananea, necessitating a trip through Benson. When the train stopped at Vail Station, the brunette saw Tracy and identified him to her husband. Silverton jumped from the train and confronted Tracy. Their argument must have infuriated Tracy who tried to climb aboard the rear platform of the departing train, but missed. He caught another train and followed the couple to Benson. "On his way ... he informed several parties that he intended to kill the couple on sight."[48]

After arriving in Benson, the Silvertons checked into the Virginia Hotel. While standing on the hotel porch the next morning, with a clear view of the depot, Silverton spied Tracy waiting beside the train bound for Bisbee. He hurried back into the hotel and asked hotel proprietor, Eduardo Castaneda, for a gun. Instead, Casteneda contacted Arizona Ranger Lieutenant Harry Wheeler, who was eating breakfast at the hotel.

Castaneda took Wheeler to the Silvertons. "... he told me that this man Tracy had followed them and was waiting for them with a gun in his pocket. This man had threatened to kill them previously, that they wished to leave, but were afraid to go to the train."

The Virginia Hotel on 4th across the street from the train depot. Photo taken before the 1904 fire burned the trees on 4th. Courtesy Bob Nilson.

Silverton asked Wheeler for a gun, but Wheeler refused to give him one. "I asked him where this man was, and at this instant the negro (sic) porter of the hotel came to Mr. Silverton and told him that this man was laying for him. Silverton took me down to the east end of the platform of the depot and pointed this man Tracy out to me, who was walking up and down between the passenger train and a boxcar." [49] Once again, Silverton asked for a gun, and once again Wheeler refused. Instead, he told Silverton that he and his wife should get on the train and he, Wheeler, would protect them.

"I walked up to this man Tracy, who was standing on the car step, and about this time Mr. and Mrs. Silverton started towards the train. I was then about five feet from Tracy … between him and the Virginia Hotel … as Silverton and his wife came into view. The instant that he saw me he jumped off the step and pulled a gun about four or five inches from his pocket and started toward Mr. and Mrs. Silverton."

Wheeler told Tracy he was under arrest and to surrender his gun. Instead, the sharp report of Tracy's gun shattered the morning calm. Wheeler continued to advance, returning fire from his Colt and demanding that Tracy drop his gun. Bullets volleyed back and forth. Tracy hit Wheeler twice, but Wheeler, the better marksman, struck Tracy four times: in the neck, arm, thigh, and torso.

"I (Wheeler) believe that I had a cartridge left in my gun when he called out to me, saying, 'My gun is empty, and I am all in.' I started toward him as I did not want to kill him. ... I laid my gun down and to the best of my knowledge and belief he shot at me twice after telling me that his gun was all in. ... He shot at me and I threw rocks and sticks and anything I got hold of. He repeated again 'I am all in; my gun is empty.' I knew it was empty as I heard it snap. I went up to him and put my hand on his right shoulder and arrested him, again I demanded his gun. We were both very weak, he tried to keep his gun from me [but] bystanders assisted me in taking the gun from him."[50] The reason for Tracy's stubbornness became clear later when extra cartridges were found in his pocket.

Wheeler turned his prisoner over to Deputy Sheriff W. Shillian and sent for Doctors Powell and Morrison. They tended to Wheeler's wounds, then sent him to a hospital in Tombstone where he recovered. Tracy wanted to go to a hospital in Tucson, so they bedded him down on a cot in the baggage car. The train only got as far as Mescal Station, about 10 miles away, before death claimed him. The gallows may have been waiting for him anyway. Tracy had been wanted for two separate murders in Nevada. Officials offered the $500 reward for his capture to Wheeler who refused it and asked that the money be given to the widow of one of the murdered men.

Southern Pacific hired its own "police" to thwart crime in the train yards and deal with situations unique to railroads, such as train jumpers who wanted to save the cost of a ticket. Shortly after midnight on May 10, 1911, Constable Frank Trask was making his rounds in the Southern Pacific yards. As a train began to pull out of a yard, Trask spied a man swing beneath one of the coaches "to steal a ride" on his way from Tucson to New Mexico.

Trask fired a warning shot into the air to frighten the hobo and get him off the train. Only the hobo wasn't frightened. "... the man demanded of Trask to show his authority and asked if he was the yard watchman. The officer exhibited his star to the hobo who then remarked, 'You are only a constable here,' and started to run away."[51]

The next day, the *Bisbee Daily Review* claimed that the unknown assailant pulled his gun saying that he "would not be arrested" and opened fire on Trask before he fled. Trask returned the fire although fatally wounded.

There is no question that the hobo fired three shots at Trask hitting Trask in the leg, abdomen, and heart. The shot to the heart proved fatal. Trask also fired at the hobo and hit him through the back into a lung. Although seriously wounded, the hobo fled. The shots, however, had alerted railroad workers who rushed to the scene and captured the hobo who hadn't gotten too far down the tracks because of his injuries. The hobo was treated on the scene for his wound, then taken to Tombstone. He identified himself as Boyd Smith "... although letters found upon his person give an entirely different name."[52] The court calendar in January 1912 lists "John Smith alias Ryneux charged with the killing of Frank Trask at Benson last summer." Note the change in Mr. Smith's first name.

The scenario did raise questions, however, about who fired first. Smith claimed Trask fired at him first and he returned fire in self-defense. Smith was hit in the back, in the act of fleeing. Did he flee after the verbal confrontation and then turn and open fire in response to Trask's shooting at him to stop him? Or did Trask manage to get off a round as Smith was fleeing after Smith had fatally wounded him?

Several lawmen had been wounded in Benson, but Frank Trask was "the first Benson lawman to die in the line of duty."[53]

His death stirred the community. The *Bisbee Daily Review* claimed that a few "hotheads" wanted to lynch Smith. They did not prevail. By now, "law and order" had replaced vigilante justice. Until 1924, however, Benson did not have its own police department. Peace in Benson remained the job of constables, deputy sheriffs, Arizona Rangers, and the railroad police.

The bad boys would continue doing their dastardly deeds, of course, as they do in any town or city in any time period. But the wild days of the Old West were drawing to a close as towns grew into permanency with a larger stable population.

Chapter 5

The 1880s: Growing Up

A visitor to 21st century Benson finds a sleepy little town with the railroad still bisecting it east of 4th Street. Union Pacific Railroad instead of Southern Pacific owns the only line through town, although with two tracks, one for eastbound trains, the other for westbound. Trains rumble through daily with whistles blowing to warn of their approach. Rumble through they do; only the Amtrak trains stop. For Amtrak to stop, a passenger must purchase a ticket in advance so the engineer knows he has a pickup. The picturesque train depot on 4th Street built in 2000 as a duplicate of the original depot offers visitors a glimpse into

Benson's original train station. Courtesy Edward Ellsworth.

The original train station was moved in 1975. It burned in 1978 from suspected arson. The duplicate station on the original site was built in 2000 and houses the city's Visitor Center.

the past, but it does not function as a depot. It houses a Visitor Center run by the City of Benson. Instead, passengers wait at a small, simple covered shelter, much like those at bus stops, adjacent to the tracks on Huachuca.

Usually, only a couple of cars park in the lots on either side of the Visitor Center. Most of the once-thriving businesses across the street have closed; a few doors belonging to new businesses remain open. Cars huddle close to the historic Horseshoe Café, but vacant spots often line the rest of the street. 4th Street is just not a busy main street anymore. The quietness of Benson in the present belies its past as the thriving railroad center it once was.

How different the town appeared back in the early 1880s! Multiple passenger trains arriving and departing through the day kept the station busy. Baggage men unloaded freight and traveling bags for arriving passengers, then turned around and filled the space with baggage from the departing passengers. Porters delivered belongings to and from the train. Conductors helped passengers descend the steep steps of the rail car while other passengers waited to board. Passengers bought their tickets inside the depot or waited with friends or family exchanging a tearful goodbye or a joyous welcome.

4th Street bustled too. Passengers scurried to and from hotels and restaurants and saloons across the dirt road. Stagecoaches arrived to exchange passengers with trains arriving from east and west. Freight wagons brought processed ore to be shipped, then were loaded up with coke to fuel the smelters for the return trip. Cattlemen drove their herds to the stockyards to await shipment and dropped by stores to stock up on supplies. Farmers brought their produce to town to sell locally to stores and restaurants or to ship to other towns. Thus the town filled daily with travelers, miners, cowboys, and farmers. "... in 1882 it was an all-night place with 13 saloons. There were eight livery stables, and they had to pile wood up on the side to keep the bullets out. There were forty trains through here every night. It was the biggest station on the S.P. road."[54]

And the building! By 1882, Southern Pacific had constructed the train depot, a freight station, a roundhouse, and

Looking down 4th Street from the Virginia Hotel during Benson's earliest days before fires burned the trees. Courtesy Bob Nilson.

a turn-style. The San Pedro Valley was considered one of the most difficult grades in the country. Trains needed extra locomotives to push them up the steep hills out of Benson. Eight wood-frame stalls in the roundhouse accommodated the extra locomotives for servicing or storage; the turn-style allowed workers to turn the engines to face whichever direction they were needed.

While Southern Pacific gave the mining companies a needed outlet for their ores, the tedious process of moving the ores to Benson frustrated mine owners. Carting the ore by horse or oxen or mule teams in wagons over rough roads took time and strenuous labor, especially over the mountains from Bisbee. And as production in the mines increased, wagons could not move fast enough to keep up with the output of ore. Owners wanted the railroad at their doorstep.

So while Southern Pacific was still in the process of building its depot, offices, freight house, machine shops, and roundhouse, construction began on another railroad in Benson. The New Mexico & Arizona Railroad began laying track in 1881 to connect Benson with Fairbank, then west to the Sonoran Railroad at Nogales which in turn connected to the seaport of Guaymas, Mexico, allowing access to the Atlantic Ocean. In its early days, the station at Nogales straddled the international boundary, with half of the station in each country. Fairbank became another important and busy railroad town. While the line did not reach directly to Bisbee and Tombstone, it greatly shortened the time and distance it took to get the ore to the railway or to receive supplies. It also provided the option of shipping by rail north to Benson or south to Mexico and the ocean. The line to Nogales was completed in October 1882.

Passengers, too, benefited from the new line. Those going to Tombstone or Bisbee took the train to Fairbank, and then switched to a stagecoach for the remainder of the trip or vice-versa. The trip was faster, safer, and less difficult than taking a stagecoach all the way to or from Benson. At Fairbank, the New Mexico & Arizona Railroad turned west serving stations in the towns of Elgin, Sonoita, Patagonia, and Calabasas, and then turned south to Nogales. Access to Mexico and towns along the route increased the flow of traffic through Benson because, during the early 1880s, it was the only train route available. Other railroad lines would later be built directly from Tucson eliminating the need to go through Benson.

The East Benson station.
Courtesy San Pedro Valley Arts & Historical Society.

Of course, the New Mexico & Arizona Railroad needed its own depot, offices, yards, machine shops, roundhouse, and employees' quarters. The company chose to build these in East Benson with an extension of the track to allow trains to reach the Southern Pacific station and roundhouse.

While the railroads were busy building their yards and a new line south, a 30-ton smelter was being constructed by Salisbury and White of San Francisco south of Benson. A spur

View—S. W. Smelting & Refining Co., Benson, Ariz.

The Benson smelter. Courtesy Edward Ellsworth.

line from the smelter connected to Southern Pacific's mainline.

The smelter opened in October 1882 with predictions that "... the business will become a most important factor in the growth of the town."[55] Local mines began bringing in their ore for reduction into bullion. By August 1883, the smelter was "running day and night with three shifts of workmen and turning out a vast quantity of bullion."[56]

By 1882, Benson's population had more than doubled. With all the construction and jobs at the Southern Pacific yard, the East Benson yard, and the smelter, the population of Benson swelled from 300 in 1880 to 820 in 1882. Many of those jobs were temporary, however, and the number dropped to 600 in 1886 and would remain there for the rest of the decade.

The *Benson General and Business Directory* for 1883-1884 listed 37 businesses. Since these directories usually charged for inclusion in them, more business existed than those that were listed. New businesses included three physicians and a druggist, a newspaper, a smelter, a blacksmith, a livery, Wells Fargo, a shoemaker, two meat markets, milk delivery, a bakery, a lumber yard, three laundries, two barbers, more general stores to bring the total to five, and more saloons. The new town put Ohnesorgen's stage station out of business. He moved into Benson, continued his stage line with offices in Benson, and opened other businesses including a saloon and a livery, feed, and sale stable. The directory also mentions a "first-class public school" in its description of Benson.

In addition to the business directory, other references in local newspapers date the existence of Benson's first school. In 1881, the *Arizona Weekly Citizen* reported that "Mrs. A. Bardick, of Tombstone, has gone to Benson to teach school."[57] The following year, the *Tombstone Epitaph* reported an enrollment of 35 students and commented that "The public school at Benson, under the management of Miss Callie M. Buster, is second to none in the county, and is an institution of which that place may well be proud."[58] The schoolhouse served the adults in the community, too, as a gathering place. Benson's newspaper, the *Herald,* reported that "A special meeting (of the Methodists) took place after evening services at the school in August 1882."[59]

According to the Sanborn map of 1886, Benson's first school was located on the west side of San Pedro Avenue between 5th and 6th Streets. Sanborn maps are referred to as fire maps. Their purpose was to assist fire insurance agents in determining the degree of hazard associated with a business property: agents set their fire insurance premiums accordingly. The maps generally indicated the purpose of a structure, such as a saloon, hotel, stable, etc. rather than name specific businesses, and listed whether or not there was fire-fighting equipment such as fire engines, hook and ladder trucks, or hose carts as well as assessing the availability of water.

The schoolhouse was identified on the 1886 Sanborn map

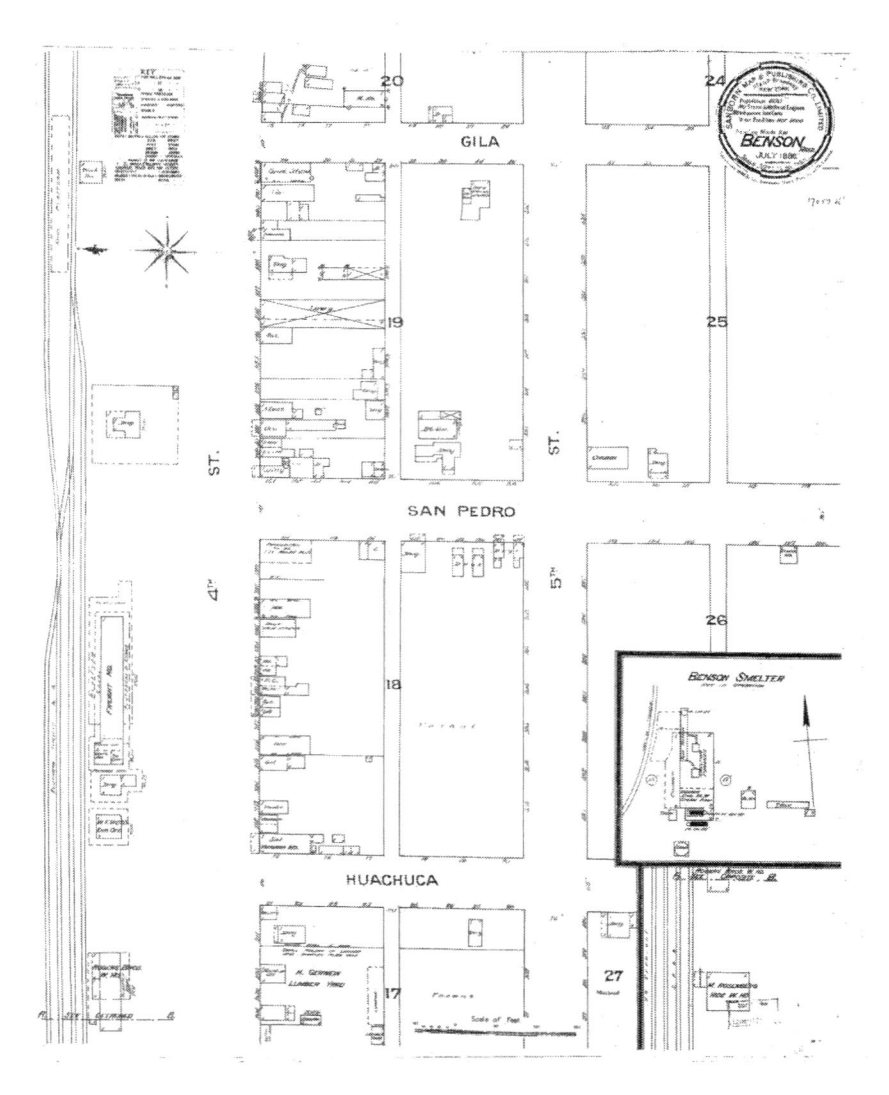

The 1886 Sanborn Fire Map shows the growth in the number of Benson businesses. The small square at the end of San Pedro Avenue is the schoolhouse.

by a small box. Since the maps were drawn to scale, a small box indicates a small building, presumably a one-room school. The frame building with a wood-burning stove housed grades one through five. The Sanborn map of 1889, however, shows the school in the same location but at least double in length, testimony to the changing composition of Benson's population. More children meant more families and a more stable population.

The legends on both the 1886 and 1889 maps show that Benson did not have any fire-fighting equipment, and the water supply was listed as poor. Although the river was close to Benson, there wasn't a water company to pump or store water to service the residents. Most relied on well-water or on Southern Pacific which shared buckets of water from its water tank or hauling water from the river. The lack of fire-fighting equipment caused major problems for the new town.

Amidst all the construction and growth and promise of prosperity, Benson faced its first misfortune. The town had just passed its third birthday when a devastating fire broke out on September 18, 1883. In most old Western towns, wood-framed stores lined the main street. The heat of the desert dried wood quickly and turned it into tinder for fire. Most stores shared a common wall, so fires spread quickly from one establishment to the next. Many Western towns burned down time after time, and Benson was no exception.

The block opposite the train depot between Huachuca and San Pedro Avenues burned in the 1883 fire. "Had there been much wind all of Benson would have been in ashes."[60] The fire devoured five saloons, a fruit store, a livery stable and house, a boarding house, the Benson Hotel, and the Virginia House/Hotel. During the early 1880s, many sources referred to the building as the Virginia House while other sources called it the Virginia Hotel. During that time period, "house" was a generic term indicating a place of business or activity as in Zeek's Bath House or schoolhouse. People lived in "residences." Whether called a "house" or a "hotel," it was the same business. After J. M. Castaneda bought the Virginia in the late 1880s, expanded and refurbished it, it was predominantly referred to as the Virginia Hotel.

The cause of the fire was labeled as incendiary. The total loss was estimated in newspaper articles from $40,000 to $75,000. Insurance claims amounted to not more than $25,000. Many business owners had no insurance or only partial insurance. Insurance or not, business owners rebuilt. A newspaper article dated October 6, 1883, only a couple of weeks after the fire, reported that "One week ago yesterday people passing though Benson saw nothing opposite the depot except the burning ruins of what was once the business portion of the town. Today those ruins have vanished and on almost every lot a good building is constructed or is in course of construction. ... Next week, strangers passing through town would never know that the fire fiend had visited us."[61]

The Benson smelter wasn't doing well. In November 1883, only a year after opening, a newspaper article reported that "Considerable fault has been found with the Benson smelter by those who have sent ore there for reduction."[62] Among other things, Benson allowed 85 cents an ounce for silver while other smelters offered 96 to 99 cents. Local miners found it more profitable to pay higher shipping costs to a smelter in Denver because of the difference in silver prices.

By August 1885, the lawsuits began and, in October that same year, the partnership of Salisbury and White dissolved. By the end of December, the smelter shut down. Enough controversy had raged over the smelter that when it closed, the editor of the *Daily Tombstone Epitaph* commented, "Times are rather dull since the smelter closed down."[63]

Throughout 1886, newspapers posted notices that the

smelter would resume operations under different management, but it didn't. Lawsuits continued with damages awarded to the plaintiffs. In December, the company was offered for sale at public auction. Notices of sale continued through 1887 and 1888. Finally in 1889, "Denver parties" bought the slag dump and struck it rich. "It is believed that the dump will yield fully $75,000 worth of precious metal, which of itself is a good explanation of the failure of the Benson smelter."[64] "No wonder the miners never got rich if their ore was run into slag instead of into bullion."[65] The plant and offices remained for sale. New owners later attempted to restart the smelter but failed.

Only three years after the first fire, another fire swept through downtown Benson in May 1886. According to a colorful account attributed to Anton Mazzanovich, a soldier in the Army trailing Geronimo through the area, the fire started in a Chinese laundry on 4th Street. "As we looked, we saw flames suddenly come through the flimsy structure of the Chinaman's shack and the Oriental himself came rushing out. He carried a bucket full of water and a tomato can. With this he was dipping into the pail and gently tossing water on the flames. He was apparently making a concerted effort to save as much water as possible, as it cost 50 cents a barrel and it was almost cheaper to let the shack burn down than use water to put out the flames. The flames swept on until they reached the largest store in town. It was an adobe building with iron shutters and a corrugated iron roof. There the fire stopped." Ten minutes later the roof exploded, flying in all directions. "The interior of the store was a seething mass of flames. Shortly after, the ammunition started to explode. Lead slugs commenced flying in every direction, and everybody had to get under cover."[66]

A newspaper account written just after the fire says it started in the bathroom adjoining Zeek's barbershop and, in another article, at a Chinese restaurant. The fire was first noticed by railroad employee Fred Clark who saw flames coming from the rear of Zeek's barbershop. He sounded an alarm and was joined by J.D. Jennings. Jennings claimed the fire was small at that point and could have been extinguished if they'd had an adequate supply of water. Instead, "... the flames spread with frightening rapidity until in almost less time than it takes to chronicle it, about a block of the business portion of the town was in ashes." [67]

Once again, Benson lost a section of 4th Street, including a grocery store, two saloons, the post office, a barbershop, a millinery store, two restaurants, and a general merchandise store. Damages amounted to $40,000, only partially covered by insurance. The cause was listed as incendiary. It took longer to rebuild after this fire than after the first one. More than two months later, re-construction was still in progress. "Benson is rising from its ashes in better shape, and a neater and more permanent class of buildings are being constructed. Nearly all the merchants who were recently burned out are now about to re-open or have already done so."[68]

With attention given to rebuilding after a fire, little notice was paid to the remnants left in the dirt streets. While the wood buildings burnt, the nails holding them together did not. The amount of discarded nails increased with each fire. This may not have been too much of a problem for the horse and buggy, but it took its toll when automobiles arrived and all those rusty nails found their way into tires. Before the Arizona State Highway Department paved 4th Street decades later, a truck with a huge magnet swept the street and picked up an estimated one ton of nails and metal.

A year after the second fire, another misfortune struck. A 7.2-7.4 earthquake rocked the San Pedro Valley on May 3, 1887.

Newspapers ran stories from the exaggerated to the understated about the damages. Some reported that mountain peaks crumbled as others erupted into blazing volcanoes, and that the Huachuca and Whetstone Mountains spewed lava and smoke that could be seen from the streets of Benson. While friction from falling rock did cause fires in the mountains, no lava came spewing down the mountainside. On the other hand, some reports dismissed the damages as minimal in the Benson area: cracks in adobe walls, possessions falling and breaking, a bloody scalp for Mrs. Fountain when a falling brick hit her on the head, and a locomotive being pushed back and forth on the track like a child playing with a toy. Damages amounted to more than that.

Any earthquake with a 7.* point magnitude will cause serious damage. But the epicenter was far south of Benson in Sonora, Mexico, near the town of Bavispe. There, it reduced the town to rumble. Fifty-one people died, most of them residents of Bavispe. When the ground began shaking, people ran to their church hoping the heavy structure would provide safety. Unfortunately, the roof collapsed, burying them beneath it.

In the United States, the worst damages occurred in towns like Bavispe that were situated on an alluvium plain. The hardest hit in the San Pedro Valley was Charleston, a mill town for Tombstone Mining & Milling Co. Every building sustained damage. Between the earthquake and the declining productivity of the Tombstone mines, Charleston never recovered. Although further south than Charleston, and thus nearer to the epicenter, towns like Bisbee and Tombstone suffered less damage because they were built on rock. Miners felt vibrations 400-600 feet underground, but the tunnels remained intact.

Benson did not escape damages. Distant newspapers like the *Los Angeles Times* and *El Paso Times* claimed "substantial damage in Benson." Eugene Rogers, owner of the Rogers Bros.

store in East Benson, backed up their claims in his memoirs: "In May, 1887, Benson and surrounding country suffered seriously from earthquakes which continued for weeks. All the crockery on the shelves in my store was thrown off, many adobe walls fell, the Mormon Church at St. David was wrecked. Many fires were started in the mountains, caused by the friction of rocks rolling down, the air was full of dust and smoke, and the people were made seasick by the rolling ground which resembled the waves of the sea."[69]

The 1887 earthquake caused some changes to the topography of the San Pedro Valley and the river, but contrary to popular claims, it did not cause the river to go underground. Since prehistoric times, rain and snow fed the San Pedro River as it wound its way 140 miles north from the mountains in Sonora, Mexico, to the Gila River in Arizona. Excess water seeped through the soil, forming an aquifer below the surface. The accumulation of millennia of rain and melted snow brought the water table, or the top level of the aquifer, close to the surface, which explains the many artisan wells which dot the landscape. In effect, there were two "rivers," the aquifer below ground and the San Pedro River above ground. When the aquifer is full, the river flows. If the water level in the aquifer drops, the aquifer will fill first. Before settlement of the valley, little demand on the water kept the aquifer level high and the river running.

"While the 1887 earthquake had an impact on the river, subsequent human activities created more significant changes in the watershed and the river, and in flooding patterns."[70] As settlers poured into the valley beginning in the 1880s, the demand for water greatly increased. Ranchers allowed cattle to drink from the river in huge numbers. Mining companies pumped water to process ore at their mills. Farmers diverted water from the river into canals to irrigate crops. Towns pumped water for business and domestic needs. All that pumping lowered the water table because rain or snow could not keep pace with the demand. "Today (2006) the San Pedro River is normally dry downstream from Benson as a result of diversions and other water use." [71] Thus the river appeared to "dry up," although water still flowed in the aquifer beneath. This may be what led to the misconception that the river went underground.

Researcher and then editor of *Pay Dirt Magazine*, Gary Dillard, also discredited the idea that the 1887 earthquake caused the river to go underground. In a 2007 lecture at Carr House near Sierra Vista, he called the belief a myth. According to Dillard, the earthquake did affect the water table and cause some springs and wells to dry up but also caused others to appear.

The location changes of the wells greatly helped St. David. From the time that native peoples made the valley their home, shallow stagnant pools of water in the area breed mosquitoes that caused malaria. Outbreaks of the disease constantly threatened any community living on the banks of the river, including Benson. Thanks to the earthquake, some of those pools disappeared, and with them, the threat to residents' health.

Human activity in the area also fails to support the notion that the river went underground in 1887. In the decade between 1910 and 1920, Mormons forced to evacuate their colonies in Mexico and World War I veterans who took advantage of the homesteading act came to the valley to farm. Enough of them came to found the new community of Pomerere. Water from the river and artisan wells irrigated their farms. The farmers joined together to form a water company to more effectively use river water to irrigate their fields and to try to curb the flow of water during heavy rains. Unfortunately, their efforts were thwarted by the river itself which consistently washed away any dam they built.

When heavy rains added more water to the river, it caused havoc, not only for the farmers but for the railroad. A flood in 1894, for example, washed out a section of the railroad at Fairbank. A rise in the river combined with strong currents also washed-out bridges. During that same 1894 flood, the river carried the St. David bridge downstream where it rammed into the Benson bridge.

Stories from the residents about wading across the river, catching minnows, swimming, or floating with inner tubes down the river indicate the river still flowed years after the earthquake. Carl Haupt, who lived here from 1932 to 1941, said in his oral history, "The San Pedro River used to have water in it all year. It never dried up. There were actually fish in the river. ... It was spread out, it was narrow and the places it came together would be a little deeper." To cross the river, "We would have to come down to the river and take our shoes and socks off and wade in. When we got to the other side we always carried a rag in our pockets to dry our feet. Put our shoes and socks on and go into town." Locals say the river did not "dry up" from over-usage until the 1950s.

Despite the setbacks, Benson continued to grow. 1885 brought the Etz & Brothers Meat Market. Two midwives delivered about 75 percent of babies, both Mexican and American. Sam Friedman bought the Benson Hotel at the end of the decade and changed the name to the Windsor Hotel. By 1900, he had renamed it again as the Grand Central. He offered "First class rooms from 50 cents per day upward. Good meals at 25 cents. Satisfaction guaranteed or no pay."[72]

J. M. Castaneda bought the Virginia Hotel in 1888 and the

lot next door, expanded the hotel and refurbished it, and reopened it in 1889. His Virginia Hotel on the corner of 4th and Huachuca was considered the fanciest hotel between the Mississippi and San Francisco until 1904 when the Copper Queen was built in Bisbee. The Virginia boasted 25 rooms, en suite or single, ranging from $1.00 to $.30 a night. The hotel's amenities included free reading, writing, and waiting rooms, and a restaurant and billiard room. He advertised it as the "Only Hotel in Benson," which wasn't true. Locals used the hotel for social gatherings and community events.

The Virginia's most distinguished guests visited the hotel on April 21, 1891. United States President Benjamin Harrison, his wife Caroline, and John Wannamaker, famed Philadelphia clothier and U.S. Postmaster General, stopped to dine at the hotel on a tour through the Southwest. Troops from Fort Huachuca fired a salute as the train pulled into the station. The presidential party quickly disembarked and rushed over to the hotel to enjoy one of Castaneda's "justly celebrated dinners." Their haste, however, may not have been because of hunger but out of fear.

Before leaving town, the President spoke to the soldiers from the back platform of the train, a typical venue for addressing the public in those days. After paying tribute to the "battles you have fought and the victories you have won over the murderous Apaches..." he added, "Nothing has transpired to mar the pleasure of our trip, but we will breathe easier after we pass Yuma."[73] Just as the President said that, a cowboy with a big hat and a six-shooter walked up to the platform. Seeing him, Mrs. Harrison pulled the President into the train car and closed the door. John Wannamaker hid under a bed. It took ten minutes of assuring him that the cowboy was not a "bad man" before he crawled back out. The cowboy turned out to be a

Tombstone agent for his Philadelphia clothing house.

The 1880s saw tremendous changes for Benson, starting with the construction of two railroads within its first two years. Benson's economy grew with the mines and the demand for silver and copper. Despite fires and earthquakes, new businesses joined the line-up on 4th Street. The ever-growing number of hotels and boarding houses, restaurants and saloons, and available services all testified to the amount of traffic flowing through Benson. Some restaurants offered a mixed menu of American, Chinese, and Mexican cuisines to appeal to the tastes of the three largest ethnic groups. The population more than doubled. As the town grew with a stable citizenry, the less negative influence the transients and "bad boys" had in thwarting the town's attempts to establish law and order.

Chapter 6

The 1890s: Becoming Civilized

The highlight of the 1890s was the arrival of a third major railroad in Benson in 1894 making Benson the only place in Arizona to be served by three major railroads. The Arizona & Southeastern Railroad, later named the El Paso & Southwestern Railroad, was built from Benson to Bisbee because of the success of the Copper Queen mine.

Previous to 1893, Phelps Dodge, owners of the Copper Queen, had shipped their copper bullion and received the coke and coal needed to run the mine via a line on the Arizona & Southeastern Railroad to Fairbank where it was transferred to the New Mexico & Arizona line to get to Benson and the Southern Pacific. The ever-increasing amounts of copper, coal, and coke, combined with cattle shipments from Mexico, prompted owners to try to negotiate rate adjustments with the New Mexico & Arizona Railroad. When that failed, the Arizona & Southeastern Railroad decided to extend its line from Bisbee, via Fairbank, to Benson. The line was completed in 1894. Please note that this is a simplification of events. The complicated history of the railroads fills volumes of books. Name changes, buy-outs, discontinued sections, and spur lines constantly modified the railroad map. The bottom line for Benson is the growth and prosperity it enjoyed while the railroads vied for dominance in this newly opened territory. Benson earned the nickname of Hub City.

Construction continued during these boom years of the 1890s in Hub City. The bang of hammers and whine of machinery filled the daytime hours as workers laid new tracks for the Arizona & Southeastern Railroad on the south side of the depot to avoid congestion in the Southern Pacific yard. Southern Pacific enlarged the capacity of its yard to handle 353 cars and ten locomotives. They also laid new rails for the mainline to accommodate faster and heavier trains. Meanwhile, trains continued to come and go, pausing at the standpipes near the depot as thirsty locomotives drank water flowing from the large tank atop the hill near the smelter.

When a flood in 1894 carried the St. David bridge downstream, it rammed into the Benson bridge and destroyed it. More construction. The new bridge across the San Pedro River rose seven feet higher than the old one in hopes the additional height would allow clear passage for future debris. The flood of 1896 caused even more damage to the rails and demanded their replacement.

The railroads did not confine their growth to Benson. For example, in the 1880s, travelers from Tucson going to Nogales had to take the train east to Benson, then south to reach their destination. Eventually, a line was built directly from Tucson in 1906, shortening the trip and eliminating the need to travel through Benson. New railways negatively affected Benson.

While the railroads continued to expand in the 1890s, so did the town. With the addition of the third major railroad running through town and Benson's designation as a major transportation hub, opportunities arose in less speculative fields than mining and permanent employment replaced transient jobs such as construction or ranch work. Although Geronimo and his band of Indians never attacked the town itself, the town also felt safer as the threat of Apache attacks diminished after the surrender of Geronimo in 1886 to U.S. government troops. The Apaches had tended to attack isolated individuals such as track walkers, railroad workers who walked the tracks to check for problems, or outlying homesteads and ranches. After the removal of the Apaches to Florida, travel was safer. More merchants arrived to offer services to the thriving young town, and more women and children came with them. The predominantly single, male population was changing.

Women are usually given credit for taming the wild Western towns. With them came the schools and churches, established signs of "civilization," to replace the wildness of bars, gambling halls, or brothels.

Perhaps the most colorful church story revolves around Alex and Kate Chisholm who arrived in Benson in 1883. They moved from Total Wreck, a mining camp high in the Empirita Mountains in Pima County, where he worked as a blacksmith and with his wife ran a boarding house called the Total Wreck Hotel. When the Chisholms moved, they brought their boarding house with them. With a philosophy of "get in and get out," miners intended to be mobile. They did not build their houses on foundations. They were meant to be disassembled into sections, moved on wagons to the next hot spot, and rebuilt. The Chisholms rebuilt their house on 4th Street, close to the train depot. In 1892, they moved to a farm in Tres Alamos, although Alex continued to work in his blacksmith shop in Benson. Since they no longer needed their Benson home, they put it up for sale. "Until this time, there was no adequate place for worship and interested townspeople took up a collection and paid Kate for the building. It was considered such a worthy cause that everyone from the toughest miner and cowboy down to the preacher donated, but it was distinctly understood that the church was to be a non-denominational one."[74]

The townsfolk did not believe the building's location amid the saloons and businesses appropriate for its new purpose. So they bought a lot on San Pedro and 6th and hired a man to move it. He only got it into the alley, however, before he demanded more money. And there the building sat for several months blocking the alley. Reprieve came from the most unexpected quarters when the gamblers and saloon patrons offered to move it free of charge. Unfortunately, they wanted to move it on a Sunday. Minister Rev. Livingston refused their offer because working on the Lord's Day was a sin. Finally, "… a few weeks later, nearly everyone in town put on overalls on a Sunday and moved it."[75] A grand celebration of music and dancing ensued, but the Reverend had the last word. In his first sermon at the new church, he preached about the sins of working on Sunday.

This delightful story is not totally accurate. Before the Chisholms even arrived in Benson in 1883, Methodists already offered religious services, although not in a church. A special meeting took place after evening services at the schoolhouse in August 1882. "At the evening services a committee of five were chosen to act with Dr. Gregory in the selection of two lots that had been donated by the S.P.R.R. for the erection of a chapel…"[76] The committee selected two lots on the east side of San Pedro Avenue between 5th and 6th Streets, opposite the school.

One Methodist reverend ministered to several towns by traveling on a circuit. Bensonites became disgruntled either with their minister or with the insignificant amount of time he visited the town or because they didn't attend Methodist services. "Benson is without a church or preacher, and the *Herald*

(Benson newspaper) says if some missionary society will only send them some good old zealous bible pounder, who don't believe in the revised edition of the old and new scriptures, and if he fills the bill he will be taken care of, without any divvy from the missionary fund, which is the way Tucson supports its protestant clergymen."[77]

The Methodists had built their church by 1893. "The Methodist church at Benson was crowded last Sunday evening. ... The church was artistically decorated ..."[78] But a problem with it arose in early July 1899. Members discovered that the deed to the lots on which their church stood had never been recorded. Within two weeks, the Pacific Improvement Co. corrected the oversight by deeding the land to them for a cost of one dollar.

Meanwhile, the Catholics began work on their church on the corner of 5th and Gila. By the end of 1894, "The Catholic church at Benson was completed Monday and turned over by the contractor. Before dedication and use it will require furnishing at a cost of about $400."[79]

Two years later, furnished and ready for use, the adobe building with a seating capacity of 80 was dedicated in 1896 as Our Lady of Lourdes. It served the Catholic community for 53 years until a new church was built in 1948.

The Catholic Church on 5th St. surrounded by vacant land: photo from the Mejia family collection. Courtesy Edward Ellsworth.

While some non-denominational services were held in the old Chisholm house, the building was not a dedicated church. In 1903, the town wanted

East Benson in the early 1900s. The Catholic Church, identified by the cross in the upper left-hand corner, now surrounded by a decade of growth. Courtesy Edward Ellsworth.

to use the building as a free public Reading Room. The *Benson Press* of October 26, 1903 announced a meeting to establish a reading room and said that newspapers in the Territory will be asked to send copies of their papers gratis. The success of this endeavor, or how long it may have lasted, is not known. Eventually, the building was vacated. In 1916, the Benson Woman's Club wanted to open a library. They bought the abandoned building and gave it life once more.

The growing population included more children which necessitated a larger school. In 1898, a new elementary school was built on 6th Street around the corner from the existing school. The new elementary school housed grades one through eight, staffed by five teachers. There were two first-grade classes and two second-grade classes: one class for the Mexican children, one for the "white" children. The segregation continued until a Mexican father tried to enroll his boys in school. The school wanted to put them in the Spanish speaking

Benson's second elementary school built in 1898 to accommodate the increasing number of children. Courtesy of Edward Ellsworth.

class because of their origin, but they didn't speak Spanish, only English. A secondary school would not open until 1914.

While the establishment of schools and churches brought stability to Benson, so did some of its new arrivals who became long-term residents. In 1896, Hi Wo, a Chinese immigrant, bought the former Rogers Brothers store on the southwest edge of town, on the corner of 4th and Gila, and renamed it the Hi Wo Company.

The Hi Wo Company store. Mural is a recent addition.

**The inside of the Hi Wo Company store.
Courtesy Edward Ellsworth.**

Hi Wo's handled everything from horseshoe nails to grain and feed, clothing, canned goods, food staples, and has been called Benson's best replication of a full service "large box store." "My father bought grain, flour, and sugar by the carload and sold both wholesale and retail. Customers came from the mines and ranches along with the people who lived in Benson. ... The ranchers would bring in big wagons drawn by horses and buy supplies to last six months. I remember," said Soledad Wo, "they used to pay my dad with grain and hay and kind of trade around."[80] Shortly after 1903, Hi Wo added a second story, an "accident of physics," because no one can figure out how it stayed up there. The empty building still exists, but no one is allowed on the second story because it is deemed unsafe. Hi Wo was the first in town to sell gas circa 1910. He also owned a lot of property in Benson. Traditionally, customers charged their purchases in stores and paid monthly or at other intervals, but at least once a year. As the railroads moved their headquarters to Tucson, many people lost their jobs and were unable to pay their bills. They signed their property over to Hi Wo to settle the debt.

Sample ledger page from Hi Wo's. Customer sales were recorded in handwritten ledgers; customers generally paid their bills at the end of the month or when they could. Although this ledger page is from 1936, the same procedure had been followed for decades. Courtesy Kay Luzadder.

After Hi Wo's death in 1931, his daughters Soledad, Isabel, and Victoria ran the store until 1989. At the time it closed, after almost a century in business, it was the oldest retail establishment in the San Pedro Valley. In 2004, Kay Luzadder, owner of the hair and nail salon Clip, Cut & Polish next door, bought the building. Inside, she discovered personal memorabilia, some historic documents, and old retail items and display cases.

Another long-term resident Leonard D. Redfield came to Arizona with his parents in 1877 from New York in a covered wagon. He was seven-years-old at the time. Benson didn't exist when the family settled on a ranch in Redington, nine miles north of Tres Alamos. One day, "Geronimo, the fiercest Apache of them all, suddenly appeared at the door of their ranch home.

Redfield's father was away. He and his mother were frozen with fright. Geronimo was after food, not scalps, and after he received some, he rode away. 'We always gave the Indians food and they never bothered us much, although we did get frightened.' "[81]

Luckily, the Indians didn't bother him either when at age ten, he delivered mail by horseback to neighboring towns twice a week. By the mid-1890s, Benson needed a replacement for its postmaster. Redfield applied for the position and was appointed on March 17, 1896. He served in that capacity for 44 years, which an article published in 2000 claimed is the longest career as postmaster in postal history.

The Redfield home on 6th built circa 1895 in the Colonial Revival style popular during Benson's railroad era. The house is on the National Register of Historic Places, noted for its high level of architectural integrity because few alterations have been made to the inside or outside. Current owners Don and Michelle Romine have kept the inside décor as true to the period as possible. Courtesy Michelle Romine.

Inside the Redfield-Romine House. The rich reds and golds of the period-appropriate wallpaper in the foyer (left) are tempered by the warm tones of the antique wood furniture. A peek from the foyer (right) into the front bedroom with an iron bed frame. Courtesy Michelle Romine.

Many pioneers faced the typical problems of living in the hot, dry desert weather in flimsily build wood structures. Jacob J. Trask arrived in Benson just after the Southern Pacific Railroad finished laying tracks across the river. He squatted on a home site about six miles south of Benson, dug a well, and built corrals for his livestock.

Jacob rebuilt a house from Tombstone that had been divided into sections and moved on wagons to Benson. As soon as it was finished, he sent for his wife Elizabeth, nicknamed Lizzie, and daughter Laura. Lizzie, however, did not like living on the ranch and moved into town where she started her own business in her new house.

Harry Blacklidge, Jacob's grandson, recalled a family story

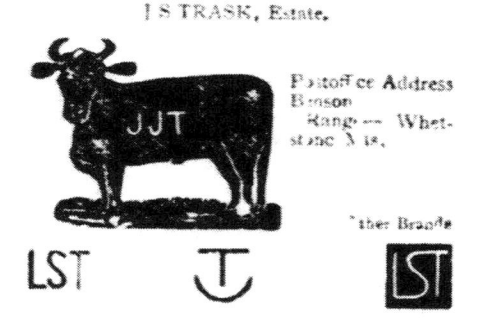

Jacob J. Trask's registered cattle brand. "Horse Brands," *Tombstone Epitaph*, October 1898.

in his oral history. "When my grandfather, Jacob J. Trask, went to raising cattle, grandma couldn't sit around, so she rented a room. That paid. So she scraped up enough to build on another room. That rented, too. Finally it developed into the sprawling Trask House, a pretty well-known hostelry in Benson. Many famous persons of the day stayed there.

"I think it was in 1897 that I was playing ball on the school grounds when some boy yelled 'Fire' and another, 'It's your grandmother's house!'

"Well, neighbors saved a few pieces of furniture from the farthest out rooms. The building itself was completely destroyed, also the Martinez blacksmith shop next door. The strange part was that folks were always worrying about the blacksmith shop catching fire - and then it was ours that started it. Nobody knows how.

"The old folks had little use for banks - and anyways, there was no bank in Benson in those days. So, when this fire occurred there was some three or four hundred dollars in gold in a baking powder can in the bottom of a box of dried apples in the little basement. The apples were pretty well cooked, but the gold survived!"[82]

After the fire, Jacob built Lizzie a "nice house" on the lot, but she retired from the hotel business.

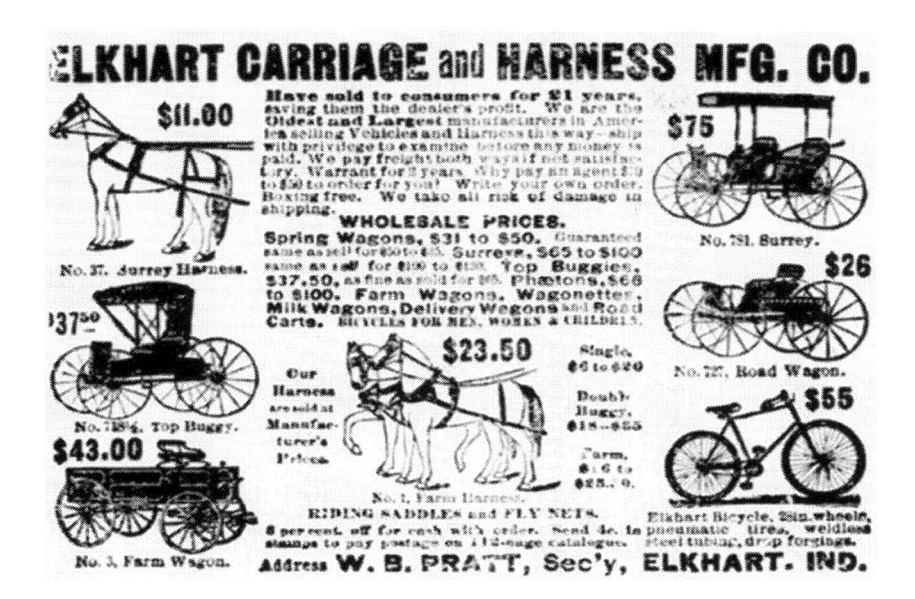

The cost of vehicles as advertised in
the *Tombstone Epithaph*, Nov. 10, 1895.

A lot of good things happened in the 1890s, but with the good came the bad. The decade started with a smallpox epidemic. It ended with the dismantling of the East Benson station complex in 1898. A year earlier, Southern Pacific had leased the New Mexico & Arizona Railroad which had built the East Benson station the decade before. A second station was no longer necessary, and it was broken down and shipped to Nogales. Although dismantling the station cost some jobs, it wasn't in itself a major calamity. But the loss foreshadowed things to come.

If it wasn't a fire, it was a flood. Summer monsoons created havoc with high winds and flooding. *The Oasis* newspaper reported typical damages from a monsoon in 1894. "The dwelling of Mr. Charles Tempel lost its porch and a part of the roof; at the residence of Mr. W.M. Zeek the chicken house was demolished and an outhouse overturned; Mrs. Callahans' house was twisted; the Grand Central hotel had a fence torn down at the back of the premises ... The cellars under the stores of A.A. Castaneda & Co. and L.D. Redfield were invaded by water which did some damage."[83]

But those damages amounted to little compared to the granddaddy of flash floods which tore through Benson on October 1, 1896. Dark ominous clouds raced across the skies from the southwest. Just as they reached the hills above Benson, a cloud burst, dropping a torrent of water. It gained momentum as it tore down the hillside on Patagonia, creating walls of water ranging from six to ten feet high. Heavy rain and hail accompanied the flood: the hailstones described as being as large as eggs.

When the water hit 4th Street, it hit its first major obstacle, slamming into the Southern Pacific freight depot and tearing it off its foundation. It washed railway cars off the tracks and tossed smaller buildings about. When the water threw a building containing hay and grain into the wall of the Wells Fargo office, it moved the office about 15 feet across the tracks. An agent inside the building at the time had to chop his way out with an ax because the doors and windows were so twisted they couldn't be opened. The storm left two feet of mud on the baggage and waiting room floors in the depot.

Hitting the Southern Pacific yard deflected the water down 4th Street toward the east end of town, flooding the businesses along the way. When it reached East Benson or the lowlands or El Vajio, as the Mexican-Americans called it, it flooded homes, rendering them uninhabitable. "Families had to leave their homes and stay with friends who had built their homes on higher land."[84] Almost the entire town was underwater.

Miles of track were either washed away or buried under several feet of hail on the flat southeast of town, shutting down the railroad for several days. *The Coconino Weekly* reported the storm in its Sunday, October 22, 1896 issue. "Few Southern countries can boast of having glaciers, yet Benson just now, enjoys that distinction. Arizona has always from time immemorial been called the land of sunshine, but now must lose all such popularity and ancient fame and for some time, at least, claim kinship to the Alpines. ... One result of the hailstorm at Benson Thursday, Oct. 1, one mile south of town, is as perfect a glacier as ever slid down any of the famed European hillsides. In this flat south of Benson, the mass of hail gathered and was washed along till it came to the railroad grade and, having no outlet, there is lodged. It covers several hundred acres and is all the way from two to ten feet deep of solid hail and ice."

But the worst damage from this demonical storm happened at the beginning. As the storm approached, Annie Ashburn, a young mother of 23, packed up her two children, Della May and Rubie, ages three and one, and headed for her neighbor's house. Nellie Zeek, age 26, and her sons Edgar and Clyde, ages five and two, welcomed them in. Together the mothers hoped to ride out the storm and keep the children safe and calm.

The Zeek's little frame house sat on the corner of 4th and Patagonia Streets. Like many dwellings in early Benson, it was a portable house, broken into pieces, moved, and reassembled without a foundation, thus not having an anchor to support it. When the cloudburst sent a wall of water crashing down the hillside, the first residence in its path was the Zeek home, which received the full force of the furious water. It broke the house apart and carried the women and children with it on its rampage through town.

Horrified townsfolk watched helplessly as the victims washed down the street. William Zeek, at work in his barbershop on 4th, had to be physically restrained from wading out into the churning water trying to reach Nellie, Edgar, and Clyde, or he, too, would have been swept away. All the bodies were found days later as the glacier melted, although not at the same time nor in the same place. They were intact and preserved by the frozen ground on the same flat outside of town where the tracks were buried. All were laid to rest in the Seventh Street Cemetery.

Had Mrs. Zeek gone to Mrs. Ashburn's house, instead of the other way around, the story would have ended quite differently. While not a trace of the Zeek home remained after the storm, the Ashburn home was untouched.

Chapter 7

The 1900s: Hitting the Heights

"The traveler gazed across the dirt road to the south where town buildings huddled wall-to-wall along the unpaved main street. There were some adobe and stuccoed buildings here and there, but most were wooden structures, a few with overhanging front roofs shading the board sidewalks. On the depot side, along the tracks were the usual railroad sheds and a large freight warehouse. Rough shacks stood north of the tracks along another dirt road. These were obviously housing for the railroad workers and their families. A large white building could be seen through the sparse mesquite and shade trees to the northeast."[85] Thus began an article about Dr. Charles S. Powell as he stepped off the train at the Benson station in 1903.

The large white building was the brothel, run by a husband-wife team. Except for structures in the Southern Pacific yard, it was the only large building north of the tracks at that time and a welcome treat to all the cowboys, miners, and railroad men looking for a bit of fun and female companionship.

"The brothel also contained a dance hall and gambling tables. On the east side of the building stood six individual cribs, small house-like structures. Between the cribs and the main building, a bar predominated and on the north, eating facilities. Big wooden porches covered two sides, and each porch was screened with vine-covered trellises. The girls, in their long silk kimonos, could be seen sitting on the rambling porches during the morning hours.

"The town folk didn't mix socially with the girls from the red-light district. They were novelties to be looked at and otherwise avoided, but when the Madame died in the early 1900s, one of the biggest and most elaborate funerals ever held in Benson took place. The funeral services were attended by only three women, and an overflowing congregation of men."[86]

After the wife's death, the brothel remained open for another twenty years or so until the law no longer turned a blind eye toward "legalized prostitution." The girls left, but the house remained, and with care and remodeling by several new owners, survived into the next century. When the girls left, the house became a novelty as they once had been.

As mentioned earlier in this book, the brothel was "the swingingest place in town" and voices and music, laughter, and loud hoots and hollers carried to the downtown. With young men drinking and competing with one another over the gambling tables or the girls, brawls were common, but no one was known to have been seriously injured there. The same could not be said for the saloons in town. Despite the continuing efforts to gentrify Benson, the population in 1901 was still predominately single males. Miners and cowboys still came to town to fetch supplies or relax; men worked on the railroad or other construction projects. The town's saloons and gambling halls continued to thrive, as did the violence associated with them.

Neither the brothel nor the gunplay interested the newly-arrived Dr. Charles S. Powell, and he turned his attention to the south side of town. He crossed 4th Street, or Main Street, and registered for the night at the Virginia Hotel. He'd soon be back on the train to continue his trip to Tucson. At the hotel, however, he met Stephen Roemer, a prominent Benson resident, who explained that the town needed another doctor with its ever-growing population and persuaded Dr. Powell to make Benson his home instead of Tucson. The doctor set up a practice and stayed in Benson until 1929.

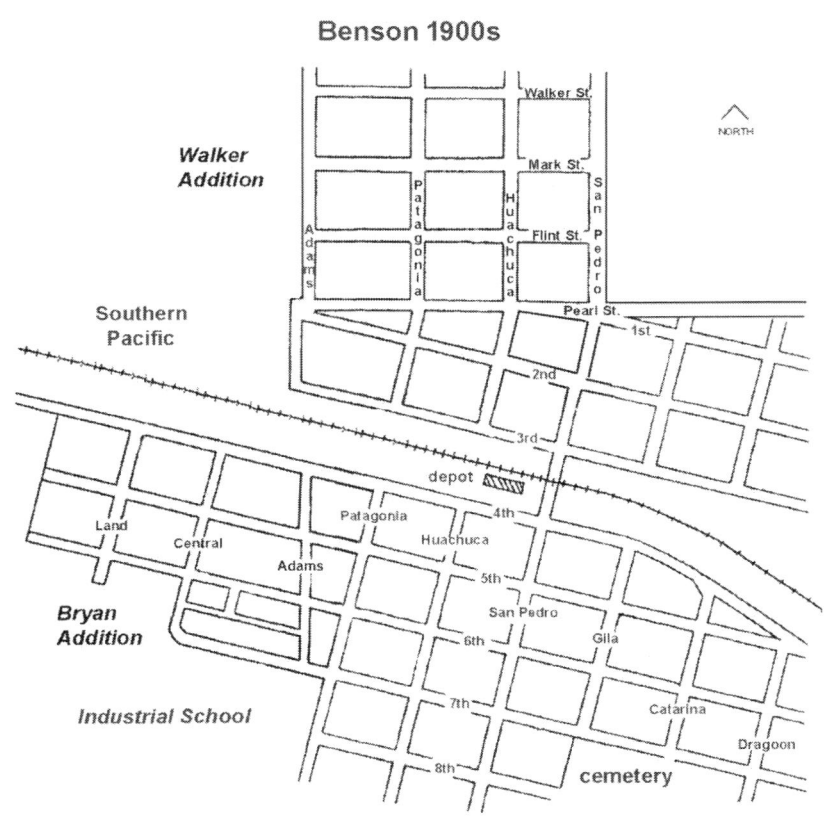

Benson 1900s

Map grid is based on 1931 Sanborn Fire Map.

Not only had Benson's population nearly tripled by the early 1900s, the town itself had grown to meet the needs of its residents. The town expanded geographically beyond its original 160 acres. The Walker Addition expanded the town north and west of its original boundaries, the Bryan Addition south and west. North of the railroad tracks, the Walker Addition added Pearl, Flint, Mark, and Walker Streets north of First Street, and Adams Avenue west of Patagonia. Adams Avenue continued on the other side of the railroad tracks, but not across them, into the Bryan Addition which added two more avenues: Central and Land on the west side. The avenues bisected the original streets: 4th, 5th, 6th, and 7th.

The additions allowed expansion for both housing and business. Two banks were established in Benson by 1905: the Citizens' Bank and the Bank of Benson. From 1902 to 1907, plans were underway for a new copper smelter to be built east of town. Much attention was given to the building of the smelter and the expected prosperity it would bring to Benson. Legal problems and several changes of ownership delayed the smelter's progress. There are hundreds of newspaper articles between 1902–1910 that covered the misadventures. The smelter finally opened in 1907 with little fanfare. A year later, the *Daily Arizona Silver Belt* reported that "The Benson Smelter is ... idle, but [it] was never a success."[90] Some attempts were made for the smelter to resume operations in 1909 but its lack of success continued.

While the town needed all types of businesses and services, some were not always welcomed by the general populace. The newspaper reported the growth of a business with an unsavory reputation in 1903. "One of the Chinese restaurants in town is becoming a noted opium den, and women are known to go there to hit the pipe. There are some things we can tolerate, but an opium joint in Benson shall not exist."[91]

What the town did tolerate was the establishment of schools and churches which always brought stability to a town. The Methodists had built their church by 1893 and the Catholics in

1894. A community of Presbyterians existed in Benson at least as early as 1900. An announcement in the newspaper on Oct. 10, 1900, read "The Presbyterian Ladies Aid Society will give a 'Harvest Tea' at the Library hall - all are welcome."

Before the Presbyterians built a church, they met in homes or the Knights of Pythian Hall or other available facilities. The Knights of Pythian is a fraternal organization; their hall was located on 5th Street near San Pedro Ave. The community used the Knights' hall for meetings, dances, and the like.

In 1904, the Presbyterians officially organized and bought property for a church on the corner of Patagonia and 6th. The First Presbyterian Church, later renamed the Community Presbyterian Church, held its first services in the new building on June 24, 1906. It advertised itself as a community church "for all who were not Catholic." In 1959, the Seventh-Day Adventists bought that church after the Presbyterians built a new one.

The decade brought another school to Benson. In 1901, the Territory of Arizona started construction on a reform school, "considered best in the territory for incorrigible youth," on a 40-

Average Costs in 1902

Originally printed in the *Bisbee Daily Review* of 1904; reprinted in "History of Benson," *San Pedro Valley Sun,* March 1986.

Land per acre	$ 7.20
Grants/railroad land	$ .90
Cattle	$10.64
Donkey	$ 7.22
Goat	$ 2.00
Horse	$19.08
Mule	$28.87
Sheep	$ 2.00
Swine	$ 3.14

acre tract on the outskirts of town south of the Bryan Addition. Its location later became the site of Benson Unified School District's primary, middle, and high schools. The Benson Reform School, later renamed the Arizona Territorial Industrial School, opened on Nov. 30, 1903. In common parlance, the school was referred to simply as the Industrial School. The invitation to the opening ceremonies, as printed in the local newspaper, extolled the school: "For the amount of money expended, there is not a finer building in the United States." Time would contradict that statement.

The school "is expected to accommodate forty inmates without crowding."[92] During the opening ceremony, keynote speaker Professor Babcock described the school as a place where "wayward youths will be cared for and taught some trade so as to become good citizens."[93] The main building provided sleeping quarters in one wing and classrooms in the other. Numerous outer buildings were dedicated to various trades. They included

The State Industrial School opened in late 1903. The missing section of the building in the upper right-hand corner is a defect in the photo, not the building. Courtesy Edward Ellsworth.

a laundry; a bakery; carpenter, shoemaker, and blacksmith shops; a barn, and chicken coops. On the acreage around the buildings, the school planted 65 fruit trees, 102 grapevines, 109 cottonwood shade trees; two and a half acres in potatoes and one and a half acres in beans. Caring for the trees and crops taught students husbandry skills.

Students followed a tight schedule from 6:00 a.m. to 8:00 p.m. On Sunday, they were allowed to leave the school grounds to attend church. Resident Steve Roemer was called the father of the Industrial School because he urged the project through the Territorial legislature. In 1905, he reported there were nearly 48 "incorrigibles" in the school: 44 boys and 4 girls.

While the Industrial School was under construction, the Arizona Clay Manufacturing Co. opened on Dec. 15, 1901. "Benson people are feeling much elated over the starting of this new enterprise, which promises to add much to the business of the town."[94] "The new brick factory ... will give Benson an industry that is bound to help her in the building of the town, as well as advertise her as the only town in the territory turning out material like this new industry will turn."[95] The plant was built on the southern edge of town with side tracks to the railroad for transporting finished bricks and tile. Chemists in Denver determined the native clay to be of the highest grade for brick-making. Six months to the day on May 15, 1902, fire destroyed the kilns; the origin of the fire was unknown. The plant was considered to be a total loss and was not rebuilt. In its short lifetime, the Arizona Clay Manufacturing Co. provided bricks for the building of the Industrial School.

North of the tracks and the Southern Pacific yard, railroad workers had built small residences for their families since the inception of the town. Because the majority of the homes were owned by railroad employees, it was dubbed the 'railroad district.' While Benson's other major hotels had been built on the south side of the railroad tracks, Alexander Arnold McGinnis and his wife Nora decided to build a hotel on the north side of the tracks in the center of the railroad district opposite the train depot. The hotel's main structure containing 12 rooms opened in 1907. It featured a wide veranda across the front and down the sides of the building. The other hotels in town did not have the room to add such an amenity. Later additions included a house with four units, an adobe carriage house, and some small cottages. The hotel served primarily railroad workers and travelers. It advertised hot baths in a tin tub for 25 cents: two buckets of hot water, one bucket of cold.

The Hotel Arnold bore McGinnis' middle name, but he never saw its completion as he died during its construction. Nora brought in her brother, P.G. Madigan, to help her manage it. The hotel did well but had at least one unexpected problem. "In 1910, a water line ruptured, flooding the street in front of the hotel. Town workers labored for days to fix it, covering their trenches at night with saw horses illuminated by red kerosene

The Hotel Arnold was first major hotel north of the railroad tracks. Courtesy San Pedro Valley Arts & Historical Society.

A large selection of items including furniture, dishes, and linens from the Hotel Arnold were sold at auction in Benson on March 22 and 23, 2013.

lanterns. Furious, Nora dispatched a letter to town officials. 'Red lights at night have been numerous in front of the hotel, which is anything but attractive to the traveling public looking for a place to stop. Respectable women will not come here from the depot. It is a hotel I keep, sir, not a bordello'."[96]

After Nora's death in 1928, Madigan continued as manager until he sold the hotel in 1933. The hotel enjoyed some briefs periods of prosperity under new owners but was eventually boarded up and neglected. Because of its dilapidated condition, the hotel has been deemed unsafe and is closed to public access.

In 1994, the National Registry of Historic Places listed the Benson Railroad Historic District on its registry and the Hotel Arnold as a "contributing structure." The building, however, continued to crumble into ruin. On March 22 and 23, 2013, the remaining contents of the hotel were sold at auction in Benson: furniture including beds, dressers, tables, chairs, old fashioned writing desks, cupboards, appliances, chandeliers and lights, fireplaces, and trunks as well as linens, dishes, books, and sundry other items.

Fires and floods continued to challenge residents. Summer storms called monsoons bring much-needed rain to the Southwest desert. Some of these storms produce heavy winds, downpours or cloudbursts, and flooding like the 1896 storm described in the previous chapter. Monsoons are the source of dangerous flash floods throughout the desert. A flash flood appears suddenly with a rapid and intense rush of water.

Over the years, many hundreds of people have been caught in flash floods. Once automobile travel became popular, a high percentage involved people caught in vehicles. Roads flood quickly because of the lack or sparsity of storm drains and culverts to channel heavy rains under roadways. With no place else to go, waters flow over the roadway which also results in short-term flooding after the rain stops.

4th Street in 1906 across from the railroad station.
The Virginia Hotel is at the far end.
Courtesy San Pedro Valley Arts & Historical Society.

Calmer times inside the Turf Saloon in 1902. The Turf is pictured midway down the block in the previous picture. Courtesy Ed Lee.

Despite warnings and barricades in the streets, people move the signs and drive around them because the water doesn't look very deep. While the water may not be deep, they do not think about the speed of the churning water. It flows fast enough to pick up and carry an automobile downstream in only a few inches of water. People can be caught unaware in a flash flood, but those who tempt fate by ignoring warning signs and driving or walking around barriers cost taxpayers many thousands of dollars every year when emergency services are called to rescue them. Thus in 1995, Arizona passed the "Stupid Motorist Law" which states that any motorist who becomes stranded after driving around barricades to enter a flooded stretch of roadway can be billed for the cost of the rescue.

Almost every year, Benson residents suffer damages from

the monsoon winds or heavy rain. A monsoon in 1901 washed out railroad tracks from late July to late August which affected train schedules. The railroad made changes to the line to mitigate the effects of high water and washouts. And while the monsoons bring rain, that doesn't mean a steady supply of water.

During Benson's earliest days, water for businesses and residents came primarily from wells or from the San Pedro River. There isn't any documented information on how they brought the water to town. Of course, individuals could have gone to the river to get their own water if they had the means to transport it.

In Anton Mazzanovich's description of the 1883 fire, he wrote that "He (the Oriental) was apparently making a concerted effort to save as much water as possible, as it cost 50 cents a barrel and it was almost cheaper to let the shack burn down than use water to put out the flames." Obviously, someone was selling water. Other towns during the era brought water in on water wagons: wood tanks built on a horse-drawn frame or barrels of water on a flatbed wagon. It's not a stretch to assume some enterprising Bensonites adopted a similar system and brought water up from the river and distributed it to customers for a fee.

Benson found a new source for water in 1899 with the discovery of an artesian well under the town. Another artesian well produced a second steady flow of water in 1900. "... excitement was raised in town ... at the artesian well and soon people were flocking toward it on foot, in buggies, on hand cars and any other way."[97] Additional artesian wells were found all over town that did not produce a steady flow but served the needs of the individual owners including the one found on the Territorial School grounds in 1907. For the water to be useable from steadily flowing wells, pumping stations were constructed to harness the flow of water and store it in water towers to be pumped as needed. Because of the drain on the water supply, Southern Pacific had to drill new, deeper wells for water for the locomotives in 1909.

Two water companies formed from the discovery of the artesian wells: the Benson Water Co. and the People's Water Co. They competed with each other to deliver water to homes and businesses. In 1905, "Permission was granted to the Benson Water Co. this week to lay their water mains in the streets of Benson with the proviso that the charge for water to families shall not be in excess of two dollars per month."[98] In 1907, the People's Water Co. also applied for a permit to dig up streets and lay pipe but were denied. They went ahead and starting digging anyway which led to an injunction and court battle. The People's Water Co. sold their property in Feb. 1912 and mention of the company disappeared from the newspapers. Although

This photo is not of Benson but shows a type of "water wagon" used during the era to supply towns with water. Courtesy Wikimedia Commons.

having well water piped to homes and businesses was a giant step forward for Benson, it also had its drawbacks. The contaminants in well water led to outbreaks of diarrhea and typhoid fever.

After midnight on Nov.11, 1904, sleepy residents awoke to find their town burning once more. Some accounts claim the whistles blowing from the Southern Pacific yard engines alerted the town, others pistol shots and the cry of "fire." Most likely, it was both. Once again, the commercial section of downtown Benson was burning, just as it had in 1883 and 1886. The fire began in the rear of J.W. Redfield's post office and grocery store. It burned for nearly an hour before it was discovered. By the time an alert was issued, flames lapped eagerly at the dry wood structures and spread from building to building. While a bucket brigade fought to stop the progress of the fire, people who believed the block was doomed concentrated their efforts on saving the furnishings and goods from the buildings. They saved a good deal of property.

Southern Pacific had its own police and fire departments. After thoroughly wetting its depot property across the street from the burning buildings, the company brought over its hoses to help contain the blaze. The fire was eventually contained at the Virginia Hotel on one end and the Wildcat Saloon on the other. The hotel escaped damage, but the roof and one side of the saloon were badly damaged. Fortunately, the furnishings in the Wildcat had been removed before the flames reached it. The fire gutted the buildings in-between: the Grand Central Hotel, the Mansion House restaurant and two smaller restaurants, Redfield's General Merchandise Store and Post Office, and the Turf Saloon. New owners had bought the Turf only three days before the fire. The building was a total loss, and they had no insurance.

Newspapers estimated the financial loss at anywhere from $30,000 to $50,000 right after the fire, but a later, more careful accounting totaled the losses at $23,000. This third fire brought home Benson's need for a fire department. The Benson Fire Department started with five volunteer members in 1907. The group worked with Frank Treat who managed the Benson Water Co. Initially, the department's equipment included one two-wheel hose cart and a horse and wagon with ladders and miscellaneous equipment.

The decade ended on a negative note. Annual ravages of typhoid fever and malaria plagued the area around Benson because of open artesian wells near the San Pedro River as well as the water supply in town. An epidemic of 50 cases of typhoid was reported in 1909.

One more fire gutted the Hotel Banks that same year. The two-story structure had opened in 1904 with 40 rooms. Volunteer firemen from the newly formed fire department rushed to the hotel on the corner of 4th Street and Patagonia Avenue when the alarm sounded, but by the time the horse pulled their fire cart up to the two-story red brick building, it was too late. When they extinguished the flames, only the shell of the hotel remained. It was never rebuilt.

The year ended with a train wreck three miles west of Benson on December 19 at 4:00 a.m. The train was running at 30 mph, which Southern Pacific determined was too fast. The engine and mail car toppled from the rails and rolled 40 feet down the hillside into a culvert. The baggage car and two tourist sleepers overturned as they left the rails but did not fall into the ditch. Although "two Pullmans and an observation car remained on the rails … the momentum carried them 500 feet beyond the wreckage … only prompt work on the part of the train crew prevented fire breaking out in the wreckage."[99] Engineer Tom

Walker and Fireman P.W. Bauer of Tucson, who were in the cab of the engine, were killed instantly; 12 others were seriously injured and 39 hurt or bruised. It was the second accident for Engineer Walker on the same curve; he had been seriously hurt in another accident three years before.

The population in Benson rose and fell during the years between 1900 and 1910. It grew "nearly fourfold during the 30-year railroad period to 1,100 in 1910. This rapid growth, not matched until the period after World War II, reflected the prosperity of the town."[100] Benson, however, had reached the height of its prosperity as a railroad town.

Residential Areas – Both photos courtesy of Edward Ellsworth

4th Street between Huachuca and Patagonia

5th Street looking east

Chapter 8

The 1910s: Reinventing Itself

The biggest news of the decade for all Arizonans occurred on February 14, 1912, when Arizona was admitted to the Union as the 48th state. While Arizonans celebrated the change from territory to state, the tides were turning against Benson.

The first major blow had occurred a decade earlier when Southern Pacific leased the New Mexico & Arizona Railroad and dismantled the East Benson station, thus eliminating one of the major railroads in town. Building of connecting lines by all the railroads continued throughout the area and directed traffic away from Benson. In 1910, the Sonoran Railroad moved its

Southern Pacific Railroad Station 1917. Trains ran on both the north and south sides of the tracks. The tracks on the south side (4th Street) no longer exist. Courtesy Edward Ellsworth.

terminus to Tucson which opened a new line to Nogales directly from Tucson. Before then, travelers from Tucson going to Nogales had to take the train east to Benson, then south to reach their destination or vice-versa. The train from Tucson through Benson to Nogales was 71 miles longer than the direct line from Tucson to Nogales. By cutting out Benson, the trip took 2 hours 50 minutes instead of 6 hours 10 minutes.

"It was not the obsolescence of the steam engine as much as the natural development of the railroad system to be attracted to the larger cities that eventually hurt Benson and forced her to turn attention to other sources of revenue in order to remain in existence. It was only when the Sonoran Railroad moved its terminus to Tucson in 1910 and when the El Paso and Southwestern Railroad (1913) also switched its traffic that Benson declined. This relocation of railroads was a most serious economic loss to Benson and effectively ended her claim to being 'The Hub City.' "[101]

As Benson's importance as a railroad center waned, the increases in population began to reverse when the railroads left. With the move went the jobs. Fortunately, although Benson's reputation had focused on its railroad activities, ranches and farms still dotted the valley. The decade brought growth from an influx of homesteaders to the area to replace the workers who had left. Instead of becoming a ghost town, as many of the railroad and mining towns had, Benson reinvented itself and lived on.

The Mexican Revolution in Mexico (1910-1920) impacted Benson and surrounding towns beginning in 1912. The Mormons had formerly established colonies across the border for farming and ranching. They were abruptly driven out of Mexico when "all former promises of protection to foreigners in Mexico were withdrawn."[102] Among the many other families returning to the United States came Alvah and Carmen Fenn, both in their early twenties. They packed up their wagon; they were only allowed to take what fit into it. With their daughter Eva and eight-month-old son Frankie on board, that didn't leave a lot of room. They departed in July 1912, leaving behind farming equipment, household goods, 40,000 bushels of wheat, and cattle.

The family first stopped for a few months near Douglas in a tent city set up for refugees. When Frankie became ill in September, they loaded their wagon once again and left for Benson because they'd heard about homesteading opportunities there. Frankie became sicker during the trip so they finally boarded a train in Tombstone to get to Benson and a doctor quickly. Sadly, Frankie died just before the train pulled into Benson.

Other families who had heard about homesteading also migrated toward the Benson area. Like the Fenns, many settled in Pomerene near the river and farmed the land. They supplied Bensonites with vegetables, dairy milk and cream, as well as new crops: cantaloupe, lettuce, peppers, and carrots. For the ranches, they grew alfalfa, wheat, barley, oats, and sorghum. The farmers were not completely reliant upon the river or rainfall because of the discovery of plentiful artesian wells and the development of a system of canals, dams, and irrigation ditches which better utilized river water.

While the ousted Americans established their farmers in the Benson area, the notorious Mexican revolutionary general Pancho Villa visited Benson. He descended from the train, and with him, 100 men carrying musical instruments. His mariachi band formed a circle around him in the middle of 4th Street in front of the Virginia Hotel and began playing. The music attracted a lot of attention. As the crowd of onlookers swelled,

Villa tried to recruit men to fight with him in the Mexican Revolution. Someone from the hotel came out and offered him a drink which he refused because he was afraid of being poisoned. While this appearance may simply be an interesting footnote in Benson's history, his presence in the valley was not so pleasant. He looted and ransacked ranches in Arizona and New Mexico. Had a rancher taken the precaution to lock his doors, Villa just rammed them open.

In 1913, the state decided to move the Territorial Industrial School to a more remote area in Willcox allegedly because it allowed room for facilities for farming and other industries. There was also a much more serious reason. The reputation of the building touted less than a decade earlier for its fine construction had changed. In the superintendent's annual report to the state, he said, "The main building is in very bad condition, being badly cracked, making it unsafe for habitation." Attempts were made to repair the building by supporting cracked areas with iron rods and braces, but the superintendent concluded, "... it looks as if we would soon be compelled to abandon the building altogether."[103] The school was also sinking.

The cracking may have been caused by one of two reasons or a combination of the two. One was the type of local soil which could not support the heavy building and the sinking caused it to crack. The second was the questionable quality of the bricks used in construction which had been produced by Benson's short-lived brick factory, the Arizona Clay Manufacturing Co.

The state ended up donating the site and buildings, valued at $75,000, to Benson to be used as a high school. "Benson and adjoining districts have combined to make the high school a union affair."[104]

After Benson acquired the building, it removed the second

story to lessen the weight of the building hoping to forestall more sinking. Deemed as safe after that, the town opened the doors of the school once again in 1914, this time to welcome 45 local students to Benson's first high school. A new building would replace the old territorial school in 1929, but would still use the territorial school's shower facilities. Children from outlying farms and ranches were brought to school in horse-drawn busses. Up to 20 of those students lived in Pomerene. Alvah Fenn drove the horse-drawn school bus from Pomerene. The school had a barn and corral for the horses during the day; Alveh fed and housed the horses at home at night. Since the farm did not require a lot of attention during the winter months, Alvah took advantage of waiting during the school day and attended classes himself. A horse-drawn school bus is on display at the Benson Historical Museum.

Enrollment in school continued to grow in the public schools. In 1915, school opened with 157 students in the elementary and high school. The following year enrollment jumped to 217. Part of the increase may be explained by the number of ranchers who moved to a "town home" during the fall and winter months to allow their children easier access to schools.

What more iconic symbol exists of the American West than that of the cowboy riding the range? Ranches had existed in the San Pedro Valley well before Southern Pacific built its railroad. "The completion of the Southern Pacific Railroad in 1881 changed the San Pedro cattle industry completely. Before rail transportation, it took months to import cattle by trail drives. By train, thousands of cattle arrived from Texas or Colorado in a few days, packed into hundreds of cattle cars. In two years between 1882 and 1884, the cattle population increased from 3,000 head in the San Pedro Valley to 33,000 in Cochise

Stockyard at the depot circa 1890s where cattle were kept before being loaded onto, or unloaded from, train cars. Courtesy San Pedro Valley Arts and Historical Museum.

County."[105] The railroad made Benson a central shipping port for the cattle industry for the San Pedro Valley. Ranchers brought in cattle to be raised and later to be shipped out to stockyards and slaughter houses.

Two factors helped to promote the growth of ranching as the importance of the railroads declined. First, the influx of homesteaders, particularly the large group of Mormons from Mexico in the early part of the decade and returning soldiers after World War I at the end of the decade. Both groups reawakened an interest in farming and ranching. Homesteaders raised goats, sheep, and cattle. "E.C. LaRue, an early range inspector, estimated that in 1917 Cochise County had 191,000 cattle, 28,000 goats, and 11,800 sheep."[106]

Secondly, several large cattle ranches began using land originally granted during the "Spanish period." The San Pedro

Cattle branding in the Arizona Territory circa 1896-1899. Courtesy National Archives.

River begins in the mountains in Sonora, Mexico, and flows north 150 miles to the Gila River. Sonora, Mexico, originally encompassed the entire length of the river and its valley. During the 1820s and 1830s, the Mexican government had issued land grants in the valley to individuals wealthy enough to make the sparsely inhabited land productive. The United States bought the land south of the Gila River to the current international boundary as part of the Gadsden Purchase in 1854.

One Spanish land grant eventually became the Boquillas Land and Cattle Company which became the largest and most prominent. Boquillas took over the dying city of Fairbank as its operational headquarters and built two livestock yards near Benson. One was south of town and the other to the north. Both stockyards were later torn down for construction of I-10.

Unfortunately, some early homesteaders had unknowingly filed for homesteads on Spanish land grants. When the courts upheld the land grants, requests for homesteads were denied, and the settlers were kicked off the land, forcing them to leave homes and farms behind.

While the cattle industry continued to grow, it wasn't without its problems. Periods of drought killed thousands of cattle and permanently damaged grasslands. "To prevent cattle from overgrazing the riverbanks and creek beds, ranchers provided additional water sources, installing windmills to pump underground water into troughs and building small ponds to hold rain water."[107] Then there was the cattle rustling. Ranchers knew their stock and could tell when one was missing. On the subject of rustlers, rancher Geraldine McGoffin said, "They'd just be shot. There wouldn't be a trial or anything. They'd just be shot."[108] Wild horses would lead farm horses away, and ranchers had to chase them down.

Cattle roamed free and often wandered into town because fencing laws did not exist. Sometimes the cattle put themselves in danger. "At the lower end of the yard last night a Southern Pacific locomotive collided with a valuable cow belonging to Justice Ohnesorgen. The cow went out of business."[109]

Livestock has been an important part of rural life and the economy in Arizona since frontier days. Arizona is an open range state. The "Open Range Law" is actually a misnomer, because no such "law" actually exists, although it captures the essence of the state statutes that do exist that pertain to livestock and fences. The concept of an "open range" is that livestock is free to roam and it is up to property owners to fence in their property if they do not want livestock on their property. The concept explains why cattle roamed freely through early Benson and why many homeowners fenced their property. Should an accident result in the death of an animal, the person causing the accident is liable to the owner for the loss of the animal.

In December 2019, a cow wandered onto Interstate 10 five miles west of Benson. Neither cow nor car survived the impact. The four passengers in the car each sustained serious injuries.
Courtesy Dave and Sue Allmendinger.

    As the state developed more urban areas, the open range concept became a problem in populated towns and cities. The city of Benson, like other Arizona cities, passed its own regulations pertaining to livestock. Within the city limits, Benson has a "fence out" regulation meaning that animals other than domesticated ones, such as dogs or cats, are not allowed within the city limits. The state statute calls the rule a "No-Fence District." If livestock roamed through modern Benson and caused any damage, the owner of the livestock would be responsible for damages.

Harold Shortridge recalled an incident from his childhood in his oral history. "The cattle were a nuisance. They ate our meager grass and the nice hedges we had planted. One day a large bull appeared from nowhere and startled me. I picked up a large rock and let him have it right between the eyes. He went down on one knee, then the other and then on his side. I didn't think it prudent to go to him and check his pulse so I waited and he finally got up, shook his head, and came after me. Even a rodeo clown cannot move as quickly as I did!"[110]

Ranch social life was tied in with the livestock business. Neighbors helped with round-ups, working and shipping cattle. A "big feed" for everyone followed when the work was done. Benson was changing from a railroad town to a typical western cattle town, but its heyday as part of the ranching culture was still a decade away.

As the town of Benson tried on its new cloak as a cattle town, it still bemoaned the loss of its status as a busy railroad town. Businesses were hurting. "4 or 5 years ago, the train service on the Nogales branch allowed the people of that region (*farming country centering about the towns of Elgin & Sonata*) to come to Benson, do their trading and return home the same day. One train was discontinued, however, with the result of a loss to Benson of a great portion of this trade. An additional train on this line would be of great convenience to the people of the territory served and a benefit to the businessmen of Benson. It would in addition provide better mail facilities for a large section of country now inadequately served."[111] Pleas were also made to the community to "Keep the dollars at home" by shopping locally instead of by mail order.

The town made a valiant effort to persevere. Telephone service extended to long distance calls; the first one from Benson to El Paso, Texas. Benson welcomed the first Ford agency from which Dr. Morrison bought his first car, a bright red one, to replace his horse and buggy and facilitate visiting patients. Other new openings included the C.F. Moss Drug Store, a new lumber yard, a warehouse, and the Benson Cannery. The cannery handled local crops: tomatoes, beans, pumpkins, and other vegetables. It had a rush capacity of 2500 cans per day and employed 50 people. The Bank of Benson merged with the Cochise County State Bank. The major addition, especially to enrich Benson's social life, was construction of an auditorium on the corner of 5th and Patagonia. The building spanned three lots and covered the land from the frontage to the alley.

Roller skating had become a popular recreational activity during the early 1900s. Towns all around Benson had or were building skating rinks. The fad came to Benson in 1913 with construction of its own rink. The Wright Walker Auditorium, so-

Corner store on 4th and Huachuca in 1912. Horse-drawn wagons or carriages were still a common sight on the streets. Courtesy Edward Ellsworth.

named for its manager, was known in local parlance simply as the Auditorium or the Rink Auditorium. It was a large corrugated tin building that accommodated the skating rink and a dance hall. The auditorium expanded its amenities in 1915 by adding a theater with a large stage. At first, the Rink Theater offered only live performances: plays and Vaudeville acts such as mind reading or magic, two days a week. Evening shows 25¢; matinees 15¢. Normally, only one activity was scheduled at a time. The auditorium could also be rented by private groups in which case more than one activity may occur such as a presentation in the theater followed by skating. Refreshments were served from a large booth at one end of the hall.

In 1916, George Kempf and Harold Gribble leased the auditorium and hired C.W. Gilpin as manager. The biggest change, however, was that the theater was going to show movies at the theater. "They will also conduct the skating rink when no shows interfere, and dancing will be engaged in as occasion may offer."[112] With the changes in management came changes in names: Benson Auditorium and Benson Theater replaced Rink Auditorium and Rink Theater. The new names were reflected in the newspaper ads. Whatever its name, the Auditorium served the social needs of Benson for over three decades. It was torn down in 1944.

Besides the new, the town also turned its efforts toward buffing up the old: to cleanup and keep Benson beautiful. "Benson is a pivotal point from which Good Roads Must and Will Radiate!"[113] The newspaper had a kind word for businesses or individuals who improved their properties with repairs, a fresh coat of paint, or removal of debris; groups scheduled cleanups and paint parties. Southern Pacific joined the effort by reroofing the roundhouse that had been damaged by a windstorm and replacing damaged sides of the building with new lumber. The company also painted the passenger and freight stations and various smaller buildings. A dance in 1916 featuring the Tombstone Orchestra raised funds for road repairs: entrance cost $1.50.

Dances were popular events that brought the community together to socialize. They were held as fundraisers, to celebrate the opening of a new business, or simply as a community event at the Auditorium. Dances sometimes provided more entertainment than just dancing. "There was a fellow by the name of Marian Getzweiller, a cowboy from a well-known ranch nearby, who seemed to love to fight. He seldom, if ever, brought a date but he did drink a lot. He would invariably walk down the line where the seated couples were and tip his hat then politely challenge each man to fight. Sooner or later some fellow would meet his challenge and everybody would leave the dance and proceed across the tracks to the north side in a field and form a circle with their cars and leave the lights on. Then they'd go to it. No really vicious blows were struck. Kicks and gouges but no kicking when a man was down. And Marian always waited for the guy to get up, as he always won the fights. He'd pick the other man up, stuff his hat on his head and say, 'Ya done good, boy!' "[114]

As was the vogue of the day for newspapers, unless the news was of major importance, articles did not have headlines. Most items were tidbits of information listed in a column; some columns had headings, some not. They covered a multitude of subjects.

> • A business announcement: "I have sold my blacksmith shop and hereby request all my customers to call and settle their bills by Aug 5, thereby obliging me and at the same time assuring their credit with the new firm. I expect to leave town in a short time, and request prompt

attention to the above. Respectfully, LE Wiegand"[115]

• Real estate ads: "I have a four-room frame house for sale at a bargain. Nearly new and can be moved easily. House is in two sections, sizes 14 x 28 and 12 x 16. If you want a good house for a little over nothing this is your chance."[116] Or, "Five room house $225 'to be removed' for sale."[117]

More commonly, tidbits reflected life in town: birth/death/marriage announcements; who's going on a trip or who's visiting; new jobs or positions available; and items for sale. In short, the entries functioned like a gossip column.

• "Mr. Doane Merritt went to Los Angeles last week, and upon his return was unable to visit his home on account of his daughter, Ruth, being quarantined with a case of measles. He is now imposing on the hospitality of his friends."[118]

• "Bennetts running to Benson in a car, a large tree loomed suddenly in the pathway of the machine and there was a collision."[119]

• Hi Wo returned from China.[120] He had taken his son Jose to China almost two years earlier to find a bride, leaving his wife in charge of the store. The newlyweds came back, but Hi Wo couldn't because he didn't have any citizenship papers and had to stay in China until the problem was resolved.

• "While riding to his home at the Gibson ranch last week, Bob Johnson's horse broke thru into an underground cavity, both horse and ride falling several feet. Mr. Johnson was caught under the animal, sustaining painful injuries."[121]

• Mrs. WJ McGill was walking down the middle of the tracks while an engine with a string of box cars was backing down the house track. "One track of the car passed over her, severing her left arm, crushing the left side and bruising the head. Life was extinct when the body was picked up."[122]

• Miguel F. Castaneda, proprietor of the Virginia Hotel, died suddenly at age 42 of hemorrhage of the stomach. He had been ill, but the illness had not been considered dangerous.[123]

• Dr. C.S. Powell died in El Paso where he had gone for treatment of "lung trouble."[124]

• In 1915, Perry Burke allegedly sold the newspaper *The Benson Signal* to C.L. Rucker for $250 dollars, payable with a saddle, a six-shooter, a diamond stickpin, and $50 in cash.

Sometimes, there wasn't a lot of local news which caused the editor of *The Benson Signal* to write in the 1915 edition, "There is a dearth of news this week. Even the weather conditions are not worthy of reporting."[125] That wasn't always the case. Monsoon rains flooded the railroad tracks several times during the decade causing disruption to train service. The worst storm occurred in July 1919. The *Bisbee Daily Review* compared it to the 1896 storm when the families of C.S. Ashburn and W.M. Zeek drowned. Minutes after the storm broke, the streets were running with water, flooding stores in town and washing out roads and uprooting trees in outlying areas. High winds caused as much damage as the two inches of rain. They blew in the front of the Benson Auditorium, downed telephone poles, and even blew over a wagon with horses hitched to it. The winds and rain caused an estimated $5,000 in damages.

The new volunteer fire department that had formed in 1907 ran into a few problems. "At the meeting of the Rifle Club

Monday night it was agreed that the fire bell be rung for calling the body together, five slow taps to be struck - then repeated. For the Wed. night meeting the signal was given as agreed upon, but the result was unexpected. Not knowing of the arrangement a number rushed downtown, under the impression a fire had broken out, and could hardly be convinced to the contrary."[126]

A more serious problem occurred six weeks later in June when a house near the high school belonging to W.D. Martinez caught fire. "Pistol shots were fired by parties discovering the blaze, to rouse the slumbering neighborhood, and soon afterward the fire gong sounded, bringing out the fire fighters within hearing of the alarm." Nothing could be saved because "There was no fire plug (*hydrant*) anywhere near enough to be of service."[127]

In 1914, both smallpox and influenza ran rampant through the population. Dr. James N. Morrison was a much loved doctor and lawyer who served Benson and the surrounding communities for several decades, beginning in 1905. Although he had an office on 4th Street, he also traveled around the countryside making "house calls." An "Oldtimer," as she called herself, was a widow living in St. David with her six children ranging in age from two years to 15. "I had a small income, but had to count pennies to be able to meet expenses." All was well until a flu epidemic struck and sickened the entire family. Dr. Morrison attended to them, not only with medicines, but by bringing a neighbor who stayed to help them. "When I was well enough to make the trip to Benson I asked him what my bill was and he said, 'Look here, my good woman, you just take care of those children and I'll attend to the doctor bills.' I was not the only one who received his generous help."[128]

While pioneer doctors did the best for their patients, it often fell to the pioneer women and their knowledge of dried herbal plants and roots to handle the day-to-day doctoring. In 1918, Dr. Morrison visited the Curtis home when Clea was born prematurely. She weighed less than three pounds; her survival depended on the care of her family. "Mother carried me around on a pillow and she fed me with a medicine dropper. It was in September and it wasn't long until it began to get cool and colder and mother would keep me on the oven door at the wood stove in a little box to keep me warm so that I would keep growing. Anyway, I lacked fingernails, eyebrows, and all of those types of things. Breathing wasn't easy. Grandma Curtis was really an attentive lady. I caught cold and grandma took these great big onions and she sliced them and put sugar on them so they would start to bleed a little bit and she plastered my chest so that when I quit breathing, I would gasp for air again because of the strong onions and that is how she kept me going. When my dad first looked at me, he said, 'Oh, she is nothing but a dot,' and I got that nickname and it stayed with me. The only place I heard Clea was in school."[129]

On the international front, the Mexican Revolution continued south of the border and World War I (1914-1918) raged in Europe. President Wilson had adopted a position of neutrality hoping to keep the U.S. out of the European conflict. When German U-Boats sank the passenger ship the *Lusitania* and six American merchant ships without warning, however, the American viewpoint changed. U.S. leaders considered the unrestricted German submarine warfare as a war on civilians. President Wilson asked Congress to declare war against Germany on April 6, 1917.

Efforts began immediately to build up the American military. The nation relied heavily on the railroads to move recruits and troops as well as equipment. Benson benefited during the brief revival of railroad activity. It also did its part to support the war effort.

There was a nationwide push to buy Liberty Loan Bonds to raise funds for the military. Posters appeared everywhere to encourage people to support the war effort. The railroad went a step further as announced in the newspaper: "Southern Pacific issued a call to 45,000 employees to participate in the Liberty Loan and announced that the railroad would advance the required funds, reimbursement to be made as salary deductions over a long period."[130] Only three months into the U.S. involvement in the war, a newspaper editorial reported that "Benson oversubscribed its quota of the Liberty Bond issue by seventeen hundred dollars. Enough said."[131]

WWI poster
Courtesy Wikimedia Commons

Besides buying bonds, other local efforts included a dance on Labor Day Monday at the Auditorium to benefit the Red Cross. In December, Red Cross ladies shipped "Christmas Boxes for Benson Boys" of home baked fruit cake, two kinds of homemade candy, stuffed dates, nuts, and books. As during most wars, food became scarce and prices rose, so there was a push to promote vegetable gardens. The newspaper did its part by running reminders. "Not everybody can achieve greatness, but almost anybody can cultivate a garden."[132]

Vegetable gardens, however, caused problems with the water supply. During the dry months, people needed to irrigate their gardens and tended to do so at night to give the water a chance to soak into the ground. As early as April 1917, the newspaper announced that there was no more water available for irrigation because a large portion of the water ran to waste through open faucets. Frank Treat, manager of the Benson Water Co. began running notices in the newspaper: "The Benson Water Co. has a man at night looking for water left running, he carries a pick handle for dogs and a shutoff wrench. There will be no notice."[133] Apparently, Treat's notice did not have enough effect so he composed a different one: "Water consumers will take notice that if the persistent waste of water continues, especially by leaving the hydrants run at night, we will be compelled to shut off all lines (except the fire line) from 9 o'clock p.m. until 5 o'clock a.m. during the hot dry spell. The machinery and wells will not stand the present strain."[134]

A few people took advantage of the war for personal gain. "Excess of patriotism or something else, most probably the latter, has tempted some party or parties unknown to appropriate flags displayed by patriotic citizens. A warning is hereby given that taking property of others can be classed under but one head - stealing, and subject to punishment. No leniency will be shown either because of first offense."[135] Others complained. "The war has broken up the World's Series of baseball games. Yet there are those who cannot grasp the fact that the U.S. is really at war."[136]

Many soldiers returning home after the war took advantage of homesteading opportunities and settled in the Benson area. The soldiers and their families as well as the influx of Mormons in 1912 shifted the dynamics of the population from a preponderance of single males to married homesteaders and helped Benson to grow. The population would fluctuate slightly but average around 950 until the 1950s.

At the same time as World War I, prohibition became a

major national issue. The proposed 18th Amendment would ban the production, importation, transportation, and sale of alcoholic beverages. Arizona ratified it on May 24, 1918; one of the earliest states to do so. By January 1919, enough states had ratified the "dry amendment" for it to become law, although the ban didn't officially take effect until 1920.

"Arizona is, and has always been, a 'license' state in which liquor licenses are issued to qualified individuals who wish to produce, distribute or sell liquor to the public. Arizona became a state on February 14, 1912. Ours was the last of the 48 contiguous states to be admitted to the Union. The regulation of liquor in Arizona preceded its statehood by almost half a century."[137] While waiting for the 18th Amendment to pass, Benson law officials used the existing state liquor laws to curb the production and distribution of alcohol.

Some favored prohibition, some didn't. As early as November 1915, the newspaper reported Constable John Proffitt applying the state laws. "Until Sunday Benson had the reputation of being the driest town in the State, observing the prohibition law to the letter" which was quite a reversal from Benson's earliest days. Proffitt raided a small house near the cemetery and confiscated several bottles of liquor and made three arrests: two men and one woman. The men were drunk and disorderly, but it was the woman who owned the booze "claiming she had found the stuff in a valise at the cemetery." According to Proffitt, her house resembled a home distillery because of the number of quart and pint bottles. She was released but kept under surveillance.[138]

In another instance in 1917, Constable Proffitt became suspicious when J.J. Spencer left his car one mile west of Benson on his trip from Lordsburg, New Mexico to Tucson. Spencer claimed he ran out of gas and was walking to town to get some. Proffitt searched his car and found 22 cases or 400-550 bottles of whiskey which he confiscated.

Pro sentiments ran high. A newspaper article, "Prohibition Helps the Workingman Says Mining Delegate," reported that H.S. McClusky, a delegate to a convention of the Western Federation of Miners in 1916, first opposed Prohibition but changed his mind when he saw the results. According to McClusky, "Men working before prohibition law went into effect, never wore anything but overalls and jumpers, now are wearing good clothes and have money in the bank. The rooming houses are full, the room rent is paid, the boarding keepers are paid for board, the merchants are doing good business and have no trouble with collections, and the general moral and physical condition in the communities are so greatly improved that under no circumstances would they go back to the open saloon."[139]

Benson resident Bill Blunt may have summed up local feelings in a Jan. 1, 1917 news brief when he said, "... a good way to punish bootleggers would be to make them drink their own vile stuff."[140]

Prohibition ended in December 1933 with passage of the 21st Amendment which repealed the 18th Amendment. The 21st Amendment gave individual states the right to choose their own system for regulating alcoholic beverages. On September 5, 1933, Arizona voted to ratify the 21st Amendment.

Whether as a result of prohibition, or the number of young men off fighting the war, or the gradual change in population to family-oriented, the lawlessness of the railroad days quieted down in the 1910s. Incidents were small compared to the mayhem of earlier days. In 1915, thieves entered the Martinez store by breaking the glass on the front door. No suspects were discovered then or in 1916, when the Maier Brothers store was broken into. Thieves used a ladder to reach a window 10-12 feet above ground. It was assumed they knew "the lay of the land" because they stole the best merchandise.

Pilfering may have been more the order of the day. The newspaper ran notices in its Lost or Stolen section such as "Will the party who borrowed our auto pump, please return it and thank us for its use. The Southwest Lumber Co." [141] Or, "Will the thief who stole a rawhide whip out of the spring wagon in front of the Post Office Monday at 11:30 o'clock, return it and thank the owner for its use. No questions asked. Leave at Signal office."[142]

Some thieves ran out of luck. "A sneak thief walked into S.B. Moss's Garage Sunday night and picked up an overcoat and a pair of gloves belonging to Dr. Thompson, and started to leave to make his getaway but he picked the wrong time as Dr. T and Mr. Moss met him as he came out of the office. Dr. T. held him while Mr. Moss got his gun and the scare they threw into him … fully convinced him that he was not as badly in need of an overcoat and gloves as he thought he was."[143]

Chapter 9

The 1920s: Prosperity

The 1920s brought bobbed hair, the Charleston, and fringed flapper dresses to the rest of the nation; to Benson they brought prosperity. The decade generated record profits for the railroads until automobiles and trucks took over transporting goods and passengers. For passengers, it was hop in the car and go: no more trips to the train station, buying tickets and checking in

By 1922, cars had replaced horse-drawn wagons and carriages on 4th Street. Parking was a bit haphazard.
Courtesy San Pedro Valley Arts & Historical Society.

luggage, waiting for the arrival of the train, and on the other end descending from the train, claiming luggage, and a trip to the final destination.

For the San Pedro Valley, "goods" included cattle. Shipping cattle by truck was faster and cheaper. Trucks picked up cattle at the ranch and drove them straight to their destination, eliminating the need to drive cattle to the railroad yards and having to unload, feed, and water them, before reloading them into railcars, at every scheduled stop along the way. Less work, less time, less cost.

Better roads made driving feasible. US Route 80 was one of the early transcontinental highways in the United States from Washington, D.C. to San Diego, California. Almost 500 miles of US 80 wound its way within the state of Arizona. Like other highways of the time, much of it became decommissioned with the introduction of the interstate system. Interstate 10 and Interstate 8 replaced US 80 in southern Arizona. In some places, the interstates follow the exact route of US 80; the remainder became SR (State Route) 80.

US 80 passed through Benson and changed the dirt road that was 4th Street to "a good gravel surface road" between 1919 and 1921. Before work began, however, one problem had to be addressed. With attention given to rebuilding after fires, especially the three that razed the commercial center in 1883, 1886, and 1904, little notice was paid to the remnants left in the dirt streets. While wood buildings burnt, the nails holding them together did not. The amount of discarded nails increased with each fire. This may not have been too much of a problem for the horse and wagon, but it took its toll when automobiles arrived and all those rusty nails found their way into tires. Before paving began, the Arizona State Highway Department brought in the state's electro-magnetic truck and picked up an estimated one ton of nails and metal from the streets.

With the highway came tourists who needed gas stations, restaurants, and a place to stay overnight. Gas stations lined 4th St. and repaired cars in addition to selling gas. During the second half of the decade, tourism became a significant part of Benson's economy. "Auto courts," as motels were called, thrived: Kings Rest Court, Kozy Auto Kourt, and The Oasis Court to name a few.

To inspire tourists to stop as they drove through town, the newspaper encouraged businesses and residents to make Benson look appealing by participating in a "Clean Up Program" which had two phases: "Clean Up Week" and "Planting Week." Specifically, they were urged to:

1. Clean yard
2. Clean up weeds
3. Repair fences
4. Repair walls, outbuildings, awnings, etc..
5. Mend windows
6. Make fly traps
7. Provide trash receptacles
8. Build fuel bins - stock wood
9. Remove unsightly objects
10. Remove dead trees
11. Prune trees and shrubs
12. Plant flowers
13. Plant lawn

The Woman's Club, Campfire Girls, Boy Scouts, City Council, and Southern Pacific joined forces to clean the right of way through town. The appearance of the town likely improved when the large, old, non-operating smelter was torn down in 1928.

With the cars came the perennial problems: speeding, reckless or intoxicated drivers, thieves, and accidents. "A trio driving an Essex 4-door sedan in a frantic effort the clear the St. David bridge drove through the side rails and took a hard dive into the San Pedro River 24 feet below." [144] Two bruised, one hospitalized. Speeding was a common problem. "Frank Taylor suggests that if Benson could put on a speed cop, and run down some of the speeders that pass through Benson at the rate of '200 miles an hour' as one fellow put it, it wouldn't be long until Benson would earn a reputation that would deter the ruthless speeder from thinking he has but a second to reach the other side of town."[145] Drivers took off from gas stations without paying, changed license plates to avoid detection, or stole vehicles. "From the multifarious tricks and deceptions practiced now a days by persons passing through the country by auto, one is driven to the conclusion that the advent of the automobile ushered in a new era of fraud."[146]

The state began issuing license plates in 1928: fees on all cars $3.50.

Another boost to Benson's economy was the arrival of the Apache Powder Company in 1920; it would become the second-largest explosives manufacturer in the United States. By WWI, dynamite was the primary explosive for industrial use in mining, quarrying, construction, and agriculture. The closest manufacturers to the southwest were in San Francisco, California, and Joplin, Missouri. Distance and high freight rates influenced the high cost of explosives. Charles Mills, a veteran mining man, thought southern Arizona was an ideal place for an explosives plant because of its proximity to mines and easy access to railroads. Mills saw both a need and an opportunity.

Mills chose a site in St. David, nine miles from Benson, where rolling hills served as natural barriers in case of explosion and artesian wells provided water for the plant. The plant was completed in 1922 and operations began.

The plant was spread out over 700 acres and divided into two areas: Safety and Danger. Safety included the office, power plant, and everything necessary for production that did not use explosive materials. Danger contained the "houses" that dealt with the manufacture of the explosives and packing of the finished powders. High hills separated the two areas; 4.5 miles of narrow gauge rail line ran through natural cuts in the hills and united the 140 buildings scattered through the two areas.

When the first order for dynamite shipped in 1922, Apache Powder employed 150 workers. By 1926, that number rose to

A narrow gauge rail line ran through natural cuts in the hilly terrain and united the 140 buildings scattered across more than 700 acres. Steam engines moved materials from one building to another.

To avoid any risk of a spark causing an explosion, engines were charged at a boiler located a distance away from the "danger" area. An engine ran for an hour on one charge.

The engine pictured above was built in 1923 and is on display at the Apache Nitrogen plant in St. David, AZ.

200. The number of workers depended on production needs, especially from the mines. "As the price of copper fluctuated, so did employment."[147] Apache Powder supplied 5% of the dynamite used to build the Hoover Dam in the 1930s.

In 1926, the company built housing for its employees. For single men, it constructed a dormitory or rooming house adjacent to the plant: each room with hot and cold water, steam heat, electric lights, and each group of four rooms opened onto a sleeping porch outside for hot weather. In Benson, it built an apartment house on 6th Street, and for the administrators, homes on 6th between Central and Patagonia Avenues, affectionately called Powder Row. It became the Apache Powder Historic Residential District in 1994. Bus service was provided between Benson and the plant.

Apache Powder Co. built homes on 6th Street for its administrators. The Apache Powder Neighborhood, also called Powder Row, is a National Historic District.

Workers in the Danger area were required to wear white suits, special shoes, and hard hats: yellow for workers, white for supervisors. Norm Fry worked at Apache most of his life. He said that the company kept sheep to help keep weeds and grass down around the different houses. The ewes were allowed to roam all over, but the ram was kept penned. Once a year, the ram was turned loose for a few days to breed the ewes. The old ram was mean and butted several guys and knocked them down. His coworker, Louie, decided he would beat the ram while penned with a white hat, and it would go after the supervisors when set free. Louie tried and turned the ram loose, only the first person it got was Louie.

Apache would blow a loud steam whistle at the start of each shift and at lunch hour which was heard for miles around. Mr. Davis, the Mechanical Superintendent, would call the freight depot to get Southern Pacific's exact time. After many months, the agent asked, "Why do you keep calling me? Why don't you do what I do? Set your clock to the powerhouse whistle."[148]

Despite precautions, 11 explosions caused 22 deaths over 35 years. "It was a dangerous place," said employee Chauncey T. Jones. "No pockets in clothes ... allowed one 'open' pocket ... you couldn't carry anything that would be thought dangerous and if you was caught smoking or carrying any kind of a device

A few of the "houses" in the Apache Powder Co.'s "Danger" area, spaced well apart from each other. Courtesy Bob Nilson.

that would make a fire, you was immediately discharged, immediately. [149] The death of R.N. Failing in 1927 illustrates just how dangerous. On Nov. 16, 1927, at 3:15 p.m., the tank-house containing 5,000 lbs. of nitroglycerine exploded. At first, no one thought Failing had died because no trace was found of him, but every trace of the tank-house was gone, too. All that remained was a hole in the ground. Because of the danger, security was tight. Guards at the main gate checked lunch pails to make sure nothing combustible or capable of starting a fire was brought in and no explosive materials were taken out.

Products changed with technology, and the company kept pace with the changes. Apache Powder, which became Apache Nitrogen Products, Inc. in 1990, remains nestled in the hills in St. David and employs over 100 people.

In 1924, Benson incorporated as a town and elected Leonard Redfield as the first mayor and Jesse Wien as its first marshal. The town council immediately had several important items on the agenda: improvements included city-franchised electric power, a municipal water system, and a jail. Electricity was highest on the list.

Before electricity, people had small generators in their homes run by gas oil. By 1925, electric lighting was in most homes but only on a part-time basis. A small power plant with a one-cylinder diesel engine and generator on the corner of 5th and Land Streets supplied enough power for lights from 6:00 to 11:00 p.m. The plant later expanded by adding a second engine and generator.

For houses built before electricity, wires were strung outside the house, then through the wall; inside, wiring and switches were mounted on the walls instead of inside the walls. Although refrigerators were gaining popularity across the nation, Benson did not have enough electric power to run them so homeowners still used iceboxes. Each day trucks drove up and down streets delivering ice. Since no one locked homes, the iceman put the ice directly into the icebox.

Before the town's municipal water system, the Benson Water Co. did not meet the needs of the entire community. The newly incorporated town bought an old railroad water tank and kept the pump but put up a newer tank.

The usual rounds of illnesses visited the residents yearly. They relied on home remedies when an illness wasn't severe. Serious illnesses required a trip to the doctor and medication which the doctor prescribed by listing the ingredients and the amount needed on a prescription form and the pharmacist or druggist mixed the ingredients as per the doctor's instructions. The days of manufactured pills had not yet arrived.

A sample of a prescription ordered by Dr. Yellott to be compounded by the pharmacist. Courtesy Dick Hamilton.

While most medicines were compounded, some were not. Before 1914, if you didn't know a good homemade remedy and you wanted something to alleviate a cough, you went to a drug store. In modern times, cough syrup is found in many types of stores but not back then. Even in drug stores, numerous bottles of different brands did not line the shelves; you went straight to the pharmacist who pulled a gallon jug of Wyeth's Elixir off the shelf and dispensed it into a four ounce bottle. No prescription was necessary; you just signed for it. A couple of swigs of the syrup, and you were probably feeling a whole lot better. The syrup, manufactured by John Wyeth and Brothers in Philadelphia, contained 25% alcohol and 1/8 gram of heroin per ounce. The use of heroin was outlawed in 1914; it was replaced with codeine.

**Allan's Drugs on the corner of 4th and Huachuca.
Compare to photo on page 115 taken one decade earlier.
Courtesy Edward Ellsworth.**

Bill Hamilton began working as a pharmacist in Allan's Drugs on the corner of 4th Street and Huachuca in 1941 when the family moved to Benson. In the early 1950s, Bill bought the pharmacy, moved it to 4th and San Pedro, and changed the name to Hamilton Drug. After Bill died in 1965, his son Richard (Dick) became Benson's sole pharmacist. He assumed ownership of the store in 1970.

As mentioned earlier, most store owners in Benson extended credit to their customers, and customers paid off their bills in whole or in part as they could. Dick kept ledgers of credit, as his father had before him, for over 500 accounts. During an interview in December 2010, Dick said that when he retired in 1996, "I didn't lose but a couple of thousand dollars in all those years. The best people for credit were the Mexicans. They always paid."

Credit worked both ways. Bill Hamilton found himself in need of money during the 1940s. He told his friend Vern Arnold while they were sipping coffee at the Horseshoe Café. Vern had Bill write an IOU on a napkin and lent him the money. When Bill repaid the loan, Vern gave him back his napkin.

Although the small town system of credit worked well within a town, it had its drawbacks in later years when credit cards became the norm, if one hadn't changed with the times, as Ray Johnson disclosed during an interview. One of his customers, Mr. Harlan, had homesteaded in Benson and became a respected member of the community with excellent "town credit." As the years passed, and his wealth grew, he had little need for credit cards and never established a line of credit with the big companies. So when he walked into Ray Johnson's Radio Shack, he had a problem.

"Raymond," he said, "The kids say I need one of those walking around phones."

Thinking he meant a portable phone, Ray sold him one. But the next day, Mr. Harlan returned. "The kids say this isn't what I want."

Ray then realized that what he wanted was a cell phone. To contract for a cell phone, however, companies required a line of credit and that the purchaser be over 18 years of age. The issue of credit was finally resolved when the bank intervened and told Ray that Mr. Harlan was cleared to buy as many cell phones as he wanted.

Ray, however, was still having trouble establishing an account for Mr. Harlan with the phone company. Mr. Harlan was well over 18 years old, actually he was over 100. Ray figured out that the online application didn't recognize the three digit number and was recording Mr. Harlan's age as only the first two numbers which made him 10. So Ray changed the birth date to make it appear that Mr. Harlan was in his nineties. The application was approved, and Mr. Harlan finally had his walking around phone.

A new elementary school opened in 1927 on the grounds of the old Territorial School. Courtesy Edward Ellsworth.

The children in Benson also benefited during this prosperous decade. When Mrs. Rosa Schwab became principal of the elementary school in 1922, she inherited an old building that did not meet the needs of her 200 students. Construction began in 1926 on a new elementary school on the old Territorial School land. The 40 acres became home to both the elementary school and the new high school built in 1929 to replace the Territorial School building. All future Benson public schools would remain together in this new complex.

In 1927, the elementary school moved to the new building: 12 rooms, airy corridors, steam heat in winter, modern lavatories, and a first aid room. It also housed a well-equipped shop which Mrs. Schwab claimed was "the first elementary school shop in the state to engage retarded students so they wouldn't drop out without skills."[150] Despite a small operating budget, all supplies were free to children.

The new facility did more than just provide new classrooms. The old elementary school playground had swings and teeter boards, but "not nearly enough for the number which had to use them. ... A single teacher policed the grounds at recess time to prevent fights and settle disputes, of which there were many," said Mrs. Schwab. She suggested the problems stemmed from the lack of activities to engage the students. The new school utilized nearly five acres for the playground. More playground equipment and room to run around for the younger kids, and a planned schedule of supervised games for the older kids: baseball, basketball, and volleyball. Kids still utilized the old grammar school, although they weren't supposed to. They played there and vandalized it. In 1928, all openings to the old school were closed with corrugated iron.

The Benson News which had replaced *The Benson Signal* in 1922 became *The San Pedro Valley News* in March 1928. Both *The Benson News* and *The San Pedro Valley News* continued *The Benson Signal*'s practice of including short local news items.

- "Saro Stanton warns the public not to trespass on his

place, south of town, as he has put powder charges out to kill stray dogs and coyotes. Parents should warn their children to stay away from the place."[151]

- Rafael Quihuiz is building a new store "as he can't afford to pay high rent."[152]
- "For Sale: In Benson, 3 lots and furnished 4 room house - $1,000."[153]
- "The number of loose cattle wandering over town within the corporate limits is at time quite noticeable. Tuesday evening there were fifteen head of range Herefords grazing along the railroad track near the depot."[154]
- Burglars broke into the Maier Brothers Store by cutting the heavy padlock on the front door with bolt clippers and stole $500 worth of cigarettes: Camels, Chesterfields, Old Golds, and Lucky Strikes.

As in other eras, 1920s Benson had its share of fires, burglaries, and floods. The worst incident was another flood. "The flood of 1926 was the greatest flood ever seen. Most of the

The 1926 flood totally destroyed the Benson bridge over the San Pedro River. Courtesy Edward Ellsworth.

water came down the river over a 3-day period, knocking down bridges throughout the area. Every highway and railroad bridge on the San Pedro River from the international boundary line to where it flows into the Gila River below Mammoth were either destroyed or rendered useless last Monday evening and Tuesday morning when the San Pedro River, swollen by a three-day rain, went on the most destructive rampage in its entire history."[156] El Vajio or East Benson was underwater again, as it had been in the 1896 flood. Both the Benson and St. David bridges went down, roads washed out, and residents left their cars at home and traveled by foot.

The newspaper reported that "Gerry Ioli, SP section foreman, says the fine sport enjoyed by the freight car 'tourists' during the construction of the SP bridge, is at an end. Then the trains moved slowly both ways for more than a mile. Now, since the finishing of the new street bridge, resting on solid concrete piers, trains rush over the river at top speed, and one who tries to board one of them is simply out of luck."[155]

Rear of the Southern Pacific depot 1920. Courtesy Bob Nilson.

Prohibition was in full swing during the 1920s. "Constable Jess Wein, accompanied by E.A. Brown and three special agents of the S.P. Co., found a still in Benson Thursday night last while searching certain houses for stolen goods. The still was in a house at the east end of Fifth Street where the officers found two 35 gallon barrels of mash. The copper still outfit was taken to the Benson jail and locked up. The operator of the still was not found."[157]

Stills to make 'mash' were not the only clandestine operations. "My mother ... and three or four ladies ... had shopping bags, three or four inside to make it real strong, they would go to Mexico and get mescal every month. They would get a couple of gallons every month and bring it across. They would come home and fill up the little bottles ... and sell it. They had people come into the house, not my house, my mother never did, my father wouldn't allow it, but the other women didn't have husbands, they would bring in the men [and] sell them ... how much they could drink. Every month they ... would go on the bus. Dad would get so mad at my mother, she would lie."[158]

Drinkers found a new use for the Seventh Street Cemetery. Several of the large monuments had parts that would unscrew revealing an interior cavity, perfect for hiding a bottle. The cemetery hosted an untold number of drinking parties.

Since Benson's earliest days, businesses frequently changed ownership or changed to a different location or a new business opened in a building that had been vacated. This book has not attempted to keep track of all those changes. Several business changes are notable, however.

The Ivey building with cement walls, oversized windows, and a tin roof was constructed on 5th and San Pedro. At the time, it was considered pretentious because it was a commercial building off the main street in a residential section. It was first used as a grocery store by merchant W.D. Martinez, then became the Moss Store for bottling and ice, then the Quihuiz Grocery. In 1937, Ivey locked the doors and used the building for storage. What makes the building notable is that the San Pedro Valley Arts & Historical Society purchased the building in 1983 for a museum. Many artifacts left in the building are on display in the museum as a glimpse into Benson's past. The museum was renamed the Benson Historical Museum in 2017.

The Benson Historical Museum, formerly the San Pedro Valley Arts & Historical Museum, on San Pedro Ave. and 5th Street. Originally built as a grocery store, it was the first commercial building in a residential area.

Another building which endured through the years and changes of ownership was Max Treu's Territorial Meat Co. from 1899. It became Etz's Meat Market, the K&H store, J&M's grocery, and then Zearing's Mercantile in 1972.

The Zearing building on 4th Street has survived since Benson's earliest days through several owners and different businesses.

The original Zearing's closed in 1997. Cindy Allen and Dan Ball bought the building in 2018 and reopened the store in October 2019. The inside of the store retains its early floor plan. Counters run the length of the store on both sides with merchandise stored on shelves behind the counters or in glass cases on top of the counters. The store also features a very high tin ceiling.

Both Zearing's and the museum are on the National Registry of Historic Places. Zearings is on the registry under its name as Max Treu's Meat Market from 1899.

Benson's Ride through History: 1880 - 1945

Inside the reopened Zearing's Mercantile. Owner Cindy Allen is measuring out a serving of "old time" candy for a customer. The original counters run the length of the store on both sides with antiques - and candy - filling the shelves behind the counter. Some of the glass cases on top of the counters, installed by Zearing's original owner, are 150 years old.

1924 brought Benson's first golf course, west of town and south of the highway on 4th Street. Volunteers helped clear the land of rocks and brush before a hired crew came in to landscape the 9-hole course.

David Pacheco opened the White Spot Saloon on North San Pedro after the 1926 flood and added a dance hall to the existing building. It was in the only nightspot in East Benson and earned the reputation of being rather wild.

A second cemetery, the High Street Cemetery, opened in 1929: $10 for family lots and $2.50 for single graves.

Benson had weathered the loss of its identity as a railroad town, re-established itself as a cattle town, and began slowly transitioning once again into a transportation town during the prosperous decade of the 1920s when automobiles brought travelers to town. But the struggle for survival didn't end. In the next decades, it would share the hardships of national catastrophes with other towns and cities. The first catastrophe began at the end of the decade in October 1929 when the Stock Market crashed and ushered in a decade of poverty and despair for the nation.

Chapter 10

The 1930s: A Time to Mourn

Black. The color of death and mourning, of bleakness and despair. The color chosen to describe some of the horrific events of the 1930s: Black Tuesday, Black Blizzard. The color of a decade of hardships.

The first catastrophe of the 1930s actually began a couple of months earlier in October when the Stock Market showed signs of instability. Then on October 29, 1929, a day christened as Black Tuesday, the Stock Market collapsed and ushered in the Great Depression. Unemployment, poverty, and hopelessness would follow and cripple the country.

Benson suffered with the rest of the nation, although rural communities may have had an advantage over city dwellers who had less land to raise crops and animals. A typical Benson family, the Haupts, lived several miles out of the town proper in the "country." "... we were quite poor," Carl Haupt said during an interview. "There were others deeply poor. But we had ragged clothes, ragged shirts. Some of the Mexican children didn't even have shoes on their feet. They would come to school bare foot all year, but they had to go to school.

"During the depression, our whole livelihood was based on the cow we had, the garden my mother kept, and the chickens that we raised." And what little they had was desperately guarded. Once, when a mountain lion threatened the cow, his father chased after it with an old 12-gauge double barrel shotgun. One barrel didn't work and he only had birdshot for ammunition, but somehow he managed to kill it because he had to: his family's welfare depended on that cow.

"Every home … had a loaded gun hanging on pegs up on the wall. Every home. Well in the case of the chicken hawk getting our chickens, or starting to kill our chickens, you didn't have time to look for bullets, you didn't have time to look for the gun. It was just there and ready. So my mother would grab it and go out and shoot them. We were used to that." Carl added that the kids didn't dare touch the gun without permission or they'd be "guaranteed a blistered behind."[159]

Other families recalled making the most out of what was available. From flour sacks, especially colored ones or those decorated with flowers, they made blouses and skirts. From animal fat and lye, they made soap. If they were lucky, Santa brought a little toy or "something" for Christmas; other years nothing.

Louise Fenn Larson described the benefits of living on a farm/ranch in more detail. "The first winter was rough. The second winter was better. Dad had planted a garden and we enjoyed the best sweet potatoes, peanuts, carrots, tomatoes and other vegetables. The summer of 1935, Dad went to Cochise Stronghold and bought 500 lbs. of peaches for Mother to can. We made wheat bread from the wheat Dad raised. He hooked the tractor to a large mill and ground the wheat that kept a good supply of flour. Mother made cottage cheese, yellow cheese and butter. I remember that year we had a goose for Thanksgiving. Dad butchered a pig. Mother rendered out the fat of which she made a big batch of doughnuts. We had few sweets to eat.

"Mother made a batch of soap from the fat, lye and water. The soap was cooked for most of the day. She stirred it once in a while with a long broomstick. When done, it was left to cool, then cut in bars or chunks. It never smelled the greatest, but it really cleaned the clothes. Mother prided herself in having snow white and clean clothes when she washed.

"During the Depression years, Dad always re-soled our leather shoes. He had a last to sole the shoes on, and he kept leather and tacks on hand. Sometimes we children were not too happy to wear re-soled shoes, although Dad usually did a good job."[160]

Through the 1930s, Benson maintained a population of about 900 people. Small numbers, though, meant a closer-knit community where people cared for one another. "That was another thing in those years, too. There was a lot of sharing. The people that made it (molasses or honey or cheese, for example) would share it with the people that had less to live on. We didn't eat much meat."[161]

Like so many companies across the nation, Southern Pacific cut its work force. Employees lucky enough to keep their jobs voluntarily donated ten percent of their wages to be given to those who had been laid off. The railroad collected and dispersed the funds all through the Depression until workers could be rehired. "That was just the goodness of people wanting to help each other," said local resident Katherine Darnell.[162]

The railroads suffered during the Depression because most people didn't have the money to travel, especially for pleasure. By 1931, railroads also had to contend with competition from commercial busses. Southern Pacific drastically cut its fares in 1933 in an effort to bring back business. Regular fares were reduced to 2¢ a mile during most of the year. During holidays, SP introduced its "Dollar Days" with fares reduced to "a cent a mile" for a limited time period.

The 2¢ a mile for non-holiday fares continued into 1934 with special Christmas rates from Benson for popular destinations.

El Paso, TX (269.7 mi.)	$ 8.46
Lordsburg, NM (109.2 mi.)	$ 3.97
Los Angeles, CA (532.8 mi.)	$17.06
Phoenix, AZ (160 mi.)	$ 5.61
Yuma, AZ (285 mi.)	$ 9.51

For longer trips, prices depended on the accommodations. As a comparison with the numbers below, in 1928, a trip to Chicago cost a base price of $82.80; to New York, $144.20.

Chicago (1741.7 mi.)	$46.80-66.70
New York (2398 mi.)	$87.75-106.70

Specials continued through the decade. For example, in 1937, a trip to Los Angeles cost $11.05 one way or $19.89 round trip. For the 1939 World's Fair in San Francisco, fares ranged from $30.35-$34.10 round trip depending on the type of accommodations as compared to $27.25 round trip on a Greyhound bus.

Greyhound bus station on 4th and Patagonia. Courtesy Bob Nilson.

Benson merchants jointed together to promote business in a unique way: "Throw Away Day." Merchants donated merchandise to be dropped from a plane "... in small parachutes as nearly as possible over 4th Street and any person catching the chutes as they land will claim the merchandise."[163]

When the Benson bank closed in August 1931, merchants helped by assuming some banking operations: the Fair Store cashed checks and K&H made loans. Most of the stores, including Hi Wo's, continued the practice of extending credit to customers. The newspaper ran free help wanted ads or looking-for-work ads "to do our part in combating unemployment." It also posted notices of jobs when a project came to town. For example, when road work started in 1932 on U.S. Highway 80 to Tombstone, the newspaper announced: "A list of unemployed [is] being compiled at the K & H Store to be submitted to those in charge of this new road work." A 1931 editorial went as far as proposing, "No more jobs for outside people on the highways of the state of Arizona. Have to be a voter."[164]

Bensonites tried to save their bank – and their money – through a legal reorganizing plan but failed. Over the next five years, they recouped 25% of their money in a series of dividends paid through the government Defunct Bank Office – when that office sold the bank's assets. The smallest check for $.09 went to the Chamber of Commerce.

Sometimes help came by happenstance. On the southeast edge of town in the 1930s, a county highway known as Stein's Pass followed 4th Street through town, went left on San Pedro Street over the railroad tracks, then right on Pearl, and over the hill toward Dragoon. Past 4th Street the road was unpaved. Whether it was from trucks traveling too fast or losing their brakes coming down the hill or the slippery red clay after a rain, many a truck overturned. When the trucks hauled produce, the accident often ruined the load. In one accident, a truck driver spilled his cargo of bananas. Knowing they would soon spoil and go to waste, he invited people to take them. "Everybody in town was hauling home bananas," Carl Haupt said, "all they could carry."[165]

Amy Lowry and Vay Fenn remembered when a truck of rhubarb tipped over. Amy tells of boys filling their bicycle baskets and bringing it home. Vay's mother cooked his share, made pies, and canned it. "... we had rhubarb for years, and I hate rhubarb to this day because we had so much of it at that time. ... But we kind of welcomed a good rain because we'd get something to eat."[166]

Whether from desperation or from choice, some tried to alleviate their hardships in less legal ways. A really desperate man might try to provide meat for his starving family. Large cattle ranches such as the Boquillas Land and Cattle Co. and the Green Cattle Co. spread across the valley. On occasion, cowboys found a steer missing. They turned a blind eye when a single steer went missing for they understood the hunger. However, if several were taken at the same time, the rustling meant someone was trying to sell the cattle or butchering them for meat to peddle. Those thieves they pursued.

Petty crime in town reflected the desperation of the time. In 1932, someone was driving around the residential parts of town at night to siphon gas from cars. Police set up surveillance and caught the thief. At the time, the average cost of gas in the U.S. was $.10 a gallon.

"Petty thieving is bad enough, but when one of these lawbreakers drains the gasoline from the fire engine truck, leaving the entire town at the mercy of the flames should a bad fire start, it becomes a crime of greater magnitude."[167] Fire Chief Ed Lee had tested the engine on Tuesday and found it operating perfectly. But when the fire siren sounded the next morning, he was unable to start the machine because during the night, someone had drained the gas tank. When the fire department could not answer the call to a fire at the Quarantine Inspection Station, enterprising men reverted to older methods and formed a bucket brigade. Fortunately, they put out the fire without too serious consequences.

In January 1936, Postmaster Leonard Redfield surprised a burglar attempting to rifle the office safe. "Stick 'em up!" the nervous Redfield commanded. The intruder, Clyde Murray, a transient, glancing at the ominous bulge in Redfield's pocket, quailed and meekly submitted to arrest. When it was all over, Redfield pulled his hand out of his pocket, clutching a harmless ring of keys, and mopped the sweat from his brow."[168]

Jason Gibson didn't fare much better. He also attempted to burglarize the post office in 1936 but didn't find anything to steal. He was more successful during his second attempt at the high school, where he found $.15. In 1939, John Williams, a 17-year-old from Virginia, also tried his luck at the post office. His crimes netted him $.30 and a pay check endorsed "for deposit only." Williams had left home so his 12 brothers and sisters would have more to eat.

Of course, burglary wasn't confined to the post office. Common targets included the businesses in town, especially the food markets. Although thieves were sometimes successful, most of the time, they were caught for their petty and sometimes unusual crimes. A thief broke into the Community Cash Store where he ate lunch and drank milk. Another thief stole 26¢ and ammo from the Foxworth-Killen Lumber yard. Three men entered Lee's Pool Hall through a transom window and broke open the slot machines to get cash. Another thief blew open the safe in Hi Wo's store for $3 in pennies and some Hershey bars.

"Many stories are told of stolen and stuffed ballot boxes, but it is Benson that has a unique record in having its voting booths stolen."[169] The booths were in storage and not missed until the next election.

Not all temporary visitors to Benson were transients. John F. Kennedy is probably the only president to visit the Benson area and not get too much attention for it. There is a reason for that, of course. He was just a teenager; no one knew how famous he would become.

JFK had been studying at the London School of Economics but illness forced him to come home. A friend who knew John G. F. Speiden suggested to Joe Kennedy that his sons Jack (JFK, age 19) and Joe Jr. (age 21) could benefit from a working vacation on Speiden's 40,000-acre J-Six Ranch west of Benson.

Jack and Joe Kennedy sitting on a fence on
John Speiden's ranch in J-Six.
Courtesy San Pedro Valley Arts & Historical Society.

Healthy ranch life would help both boys get in shape for the fall athletic season at Harvard; Jack in particular would benefit from the dry desert heat.

During the summer of 1936, the brothers rode fence, herded cattle, and helped put up an adobe office for their host. Speiden liked to call it "the house that Jack built." Years later, after JFK became President, Speiden visited Washington, D.C. and told JFK that when his presidency was over, his old job as a cowboy was still waiting for him. Kennedy reportedly laughed uproariously.

Joe, left, and Jack Kennedy at work building an adobe office-den on an Arizona ranch.

"The house that Jack built" on Speiden's ranch in J-Six.
Courtesy San Pedro Valley Arts & Historical Society.

By 1932, the Benson newspaper began making claims that the Depression was almost over. A headline in the August 26th edition read "Depression Has Turned." An ad for the Fair Store on August 18, 1933, announced "Absolutely Your Last Chance to

Get Your Needs at Depression Prices." The Depression would actually continue for the rest of the decade.

In Benson, however, life did improve. In 1931, the El Paso Natural Gas Co. began laying a natural gas 10" pipeline pipe in Cochise Country. Many men found jobs working on the pipeline. Workmen from out of town needed housing: houses or apartments, furnished or unfurnished, filled up. The following For Rent ads range from 1934 to 1937.

- "House for Rent: 5 rooms, kitchen, bath, and service porch. $18 mo."[170] 1934
- "3 room apt. furnished with lights and water. $10 mo."[171] 1935
- The Oasis: "Cabins to rent $10 per month."[172] 1936
- "Furnished home: 4 rooms, bath, hot water. $18 mo."[173] 1936
- "For Rent – Nice, clean furnished house, four rooms and a sunporch, $25 per month."[174] 1937

In 1933, the pipeline was laid west of Benson. Once the main pipeline was completed, towns had to connect to the pipeline. The town applied to the Works Progress Administration (WPA), a federal program of the New Deal, for funding to bring gas into Benson. The application was approved in July, 1938: the WPA granted $15,000 and the town was to issue bonds for a $20,000 loan. The town also applied to the WPA for funding for a sewer system. A debate arose in town as to which to get: the town could not afford to do both. The gas line won because it was more affordable. By November, the town had become a town of ditches and ridges as streets were torn up to lay pipes. Unskilled labor was paid 65.5¢ an hour. Drivers had to plan their routes around the construction; some cars were stuck in garages for days. Complaints were few, however, because of the great convenience to come. On

December 16th, the gas was turned on.

Meanwhile, the town had planned how to handle the business end of the gas: rates, collection of fees, bookkeeping, etc. On Dec. 9, 1938, the Southern Arizona Public Service Co. was given the job of running the water and gas departments. The Sulphur Springs Valley Electric Co-op (SSVEC), which had started a month earlier, would handle the electric.

While Bensonites were happy about the pipeline, one crewman wasn't. "One of them became drunk and decided to sleep in the women's waiting room at the depot and insisted on all the formalities of undressing. Judge Benton fined him $10 or 10 days. It took him a day to get the ten dollars."[175]

In 1933-1934, the state repaved Highway 80 through town. It widened 4th Street where possible but not the three principal blocks as the railroad property abutted the highway. The repaving included widening the curve on the southwest end of town. To do so, the state needed to take off fractions of seven lots, including the lot where the jail was. The jail jutted 6 ft. into the right-of-way for widening the curve. The town debated whether or not to take off part of the jail or to move the whole building. For the short term, the northeast corner of the jail was removed. A few years later, in 1937, the town acquired a county jail slated to be torn down, an upgrade from its current jail, and brought it to Benson. The jail was relocated to a lot on Huachuca and 5th.

Throughout Benson's history, cattle or horses on the highway had caused a number of serious accidents. While the state was paving Highway 80, the town council considered erecting a fence on the east side of town and asked Southern Pacific and the Arizona Highway Dept. to put in cattle guards across the highway and railroad tracks. The Highway Dept. did more than that; they, too, wanted to keep cattle off the repaved highway. They erected the fence. "For years cattle have roamed through the streets of Benson at will. At times they were much worse than others but at all times it has been necessary to have one's property enclosed with a fence if one wanted to grow flowers. But all of these fences can be done away with as the city of Benson is to be protected by a fence that will keep the cows out. The State highway department has been busy this past week building the fence and will soon have it finished."[176]

After the completion of the paved section of Highway 80 which ran south, Benson began lobbying for the state to pave Steins Pass and incorporate it into the state's highway system and maintain it. Other cities protested because the proposed highway known as the Sunset Trail or the Sunset Highway or Highway 86, created a shortcut from Benson through the Dragoon Mountains to Willcox and New Mexico, eliminating the long, time-consuming loop south through Douglas and other southern cities on Route 80. The cities did not want to lose the traffic and the business it brought. Benson prevailed. Transitioning from one highway to the other, however, was problematic. Highway improvements culminated in 1941 with the construction of an overpass which permitted a smooth convergence between Highways 80 and 86.

"As railway traffic dwindled, Benson's importance decreased, only to rise again in the 1930s with construction of the Sunset Trail Highway (Highway 86) along the present I-10 freeway route, once again establishing Benson as a travel hub."[177] An increase of vehicular traffic meant more gas stations, restaurants, auto courts, and garages in Benson, all of which helped boost the economy. "These construction programs concerned with repairing roads and bridges were to prove a boon to the area in terms of improved transportation. In a sense, they literally 'paved the way' for the age of the automobile

Highway in Texas Canyon - Between Willcox and Benson, Ariz.

The paving of Highway 86 through Texas Canyon brought business to Benson. Courtesy Bob Nilson.

and the truck. ... The mode of transportation had changed from the Iron Horse to the Horseless Carriage, but Benson's desirable position at the junction of east-west and north-south routes remained the same."[178]

Perhaps part of Benson's feeling of well-being also came because its major employer, the Apache Powder Company which employed over 200 workers, never cut its work force. In 1933, a spokesman said, "Our business has slackened, our output has dwindled, and we have suffered greatly from the depression, but we have never yet reduced wages. We are still paying the peak wage of 1929 ..." The newspaper called the company an asset to Benson and the state. "Any firm that has struggled through the past four years without cutting wages and endeavoring to keep all the men they possibly could on the payroll is deserving of all the praise that can be heaped upon them."[179]

Although Apache Powder never reduced its payroll, that's not to say that some employees didn't change. On his way to Tucson in 1931, Ray Kenworthy stopped in Benson to say hello to two men from his home town in Pennsylvania: one a manager at Apache; the other, the head of research. During their conversation, he asked about jobs at the plant. Since he had experience working with explosives, his friends immediately took him to the plant for an interview.

On a tour through a laboratory, the interviewer introduced him to an employee, then said to that employee, "He'll be taking over your job Monday." "The fella's face just fell, right in the middle of a Depression, his face fell about that far ..."

When Kenworthy arrived at the plant on the following Monday, the man said, "Meet the dumbest man in the world." When Kenworthy asked him to explain what had gone wrong, the man responded, "I was just asking for a raise." Surprised, Kenworthy asked him if he had really asked for a raise in the midst of the Depression. He replied, "Like I said, meet the dumbest man."[180]

Any feeling of well-being, however, was tempered as another menace crouched on the horizon. In 1862, President Lincoln passed the Homestead Act to draw farmers to the rich, fertile soil of the Midwest. And they came. They ploughed under the prairie grass and soon the fields turned to gold with acre after acre of wheat blowing in the sunshine. No one realized at the time that in ploughing under the native grass, they were also destroying the basis of the soil's richness, the anchor that kept the nutrients and moisture in the soil.

Year after prosperous year farmers ploughed, depleting the topsoil. When the jet stream from the south that brought moisture to their fields shifted its course westward in 1931, the amount of rain decreased from the normal 20 inches a year to less than nine inches, causing a drought. Crops failed. In desperation, the farmers ploughed and planted, ploughed and planted, uncovering what little was left of the fertile soil and exposing it to the winds.

And the winds blew: gale force winds of 50 to 80 miles an hour. Sometimes they blew for hours, sometimes for days. As they raced across the land, the winds took with them the exposed topsoil, whipping it into the air. Higher and higher the particles blew until dust clouds a mile high darkened the landscape and coated everything in its wake with inches of powdered dirt.

Clouds of dust and dirt blackened skies. Pictured here is the Texas Panhandle in 1936. Courtesy U.S. Farm Security Administration.

Because of the Depression, Easterners paid little attention to the plight of Midwest farmers until the "black blizzards" of 1934 and 1935 blew dirt all the way to the Atlantic coast. Dust swirled down the streets of New York, Boston, and Washington D.C., blanketing them under tons of dirt. That first-hand experience brought "home" to Easterners the devastating effects of the Dust Bowl.

South Dakota 1936. People fled from their devastated homes and farms in the Midwest. Many passed through Benson on their way to California. Courtesy U.S. Dept. of Agriculture.

More than 2.5 million people fled from the barren lands of the Midwest, many passing through Benson. Vay Fenn recalled the migration of displaced families. "We lived pretty close to this old shortcut road, on the Pomerene Road. We got to see the movement of people looking for work. They were poor people. They'd have chickens on their cars, their trucks and cars loaded down and moving looking for work." Single men often resorted to hitching a ride on the railroad. "... hobos, as we'd call 'em, traveling ... people looking for work. Riding the freight trains ... a lot of these fellers that would come, ask for work, for food. Mother never turned one of 'em down for work. She always feed 'em. They always done a little work too. Chop a little wood, clean up a little bit, or hoe some weeds."[181]

Trains slowed down to 30 mph for the curves coming into Benson, creating a jumping on and off point for hobos "riding the rails." The practice, however, was dangerous, and miscalculations caused deaths. In 1931, "a young man attempted to climb aboard but lost his hold and was slung down by the side of the track with both feet across the rails, his head striking against some hard object and fracturing his skull from top to base, while both feet were cut off by the heavy wheels passing over them."[182] The eighteen-year-old had the money to pay the fare but had decided to save it and hitch a free ride.

While the Benson newspaper did not report any problems from the dust storms, it did chronicle problems for farmers and ranchers caused by the lack of rain. The same drought that hit the Midwest reached westward into the San Pedro Valley, especially between 1933 and 1935, and left farmers with parched lands and ranchers with thirsty cattle. The drought in Benson, however, was not nearly as severe as it was in the Midwest; summer monsoon rains brought some rain.

An indirect consequence arose from travelers fleeing from their homes in the Midwest. The unsightly condition of vacant lots used by campers at the edge of town prompted the town council to put up "No Camping" signs around town. The council also ordered the marshal to watch out for campers and not to permit any person to camp on any vacant lot within the city limits.

Benson also had other local issues to contend with: measles, mumps, flu, and Scarlet Fever — all common communicable diseases before medicine discovered immunization shots. Outbreaks occurred regularly; the 1930s was no exception. In 1931, the grammar school closed for two weeks in March because of a measles epidemic and for a week in September 1933 because of Scarlet Fever. Another outbreak of both the measles and the mumps in 1936 curtailed the activities of Benson kids. All kids under the age of 21 were allowed to go to school but other public gathering places such as the movie theater or skating rink were forbidden. There was no loitering between school and home, no contact with neighborhood kids or visiting other towns. "The measles were brot [brought] to Benson by visitors from Mexico where quarantine measures are not enforced."[182]

Adults, too, suffered from outbreaks. In 1933 and 1936, Health Officer Richard Yellot, M.D., ordered the town's water supply to be chlorinated to purify the water because of the presence of B. coli which had caused numerous cases of diarrhea. The newspaper warned that the "objectionable taste will probably be noticed for some days after it reaches the main."[183] A 1937 flu outbreak was considered "a more dangerous version this year … So prevalent has the flu become in Benson that almost every home has been touched by it."[184] Once again, the grammar school and movie theater were closed.

While dealing with common diseases was not unusual, nothing scared the community more than when polio (poliomyelitis) visited Benson in 1934: at that time it was commonly referred to as infantile paralysis. The first case appeared at the beginning of August. The ranch where the child lived was quarantined to prevent the spread of the disease, but when another child became ill in late September, the town took action. Schools were closed in Benson and St. David. Attendance had been poor anyway because fearful parents kept their children at home. They had reason to be fearful. Although the epidemic was a few years in the future, in the 1940s and 1950s, polio was about to kill or paralyze over half a million people worldwide every year. In 1952, the height of the epidemic, there were 60,000 cases and 3,000 deaths in the U.S. alone.

Kids usually enjoyed an unexpected break from school but not in this case. The mandate confined all children under the age of 21 to their homes. "This means there shall be no visiting among neighbors, no coming to town in cars, and no leaving town under any condition. There shall be no public meetings or private gatherings of persons under this age."[185] The quarantine lifted a week earlier than expected when there were no new cases. "There was shouting, singing, dancing, yelling, and many other ways of expressing happiness in being allowed to go into someone else's yard."[186]

As a small town with limited resources, Benson did not have the most sanitary conditions. Because of the lack of a sewer system, the Common Council of the Town of Benson passed Ordinance #36 on Dec. 2, 1935. It dealt with the construction or rebuild of privies, describing in detail the specifications set by State Department of Health. A new privy which followed the state specifications cost $14. The Ordinance also outlined the consequences for those who failed to comply with the Ordinance: a fine up to $100, up to 90 days in jail, or both a fine and imprisonment.

On a good note, Dr. Moffitt brought the first portable X-ray machine to Benson in 1938. Before that, patients had to go to Tombstone or Tucson for broken bones, lung scans, and other ailments requiring an X-ray.

Dire as conditions were, especially during the first half of the decade, that is not to say that Benson residents did not find time to enjoy themselves: a psychological "must" to balance the bleakness. Bensonites have always loved their dances, especially when the popular Troubadours were playing. Two new venues opened for dances. One was the tennis courts on the school campus. Those, and other venues in town, could get so rowdy that a special officer was assigned to keep the peace.

The Skyline Club, a dance pavilion perched high on granite boulders in Texas Canyon, was only accessible by a staircase from the parking lot below. Too many accidents on the staircase eventually caused the club's demise. Courtesy Edward Ellsworth.

The other new venue was the Skyline Club. Bostice and Mable Williams opened the Skyline, an open-air dance pavilion, in June 1934 in Texas Canyon, a natural pass through the Dragoon Mountains 20 miles east of Benson. The club was perched on giant granite boulders 100 ft. above the canyon floor. It was reached by a series of 150 steps from the parking lot below. After numerous accidents on the rough wood staircase, the club shut down. The Williams also owned the Horseshoe Café, a Benson landmark, and the Greyhound Bus Depot on 4th and Patagonia.

The annual rodeo also began in 1934. It was such an important and popular event that it deserves a chapter all its own. See the following chapter, "Hang On, Cowboy."

A carnival came to town in 1933 and 1939 and The Barney Brothers Three Ring Wild Animals Circus in 1937. Residents watched Hollywood stars: Shirley Temple, Bing Crosby, Katherine Hepburn, Ginger Rogers, Fred Astaire, or John Wayne on the big screen in classics such as *Stagecoach, Double or Nothing, Carefree, Stage Door, and Little Orphan Annie*. Family night tickets, $1.25. *Confessions of a Nazi Spy* foreshadowed the impending war.

The tradition of an Annual Community Christmas tree was revived in 1937. Kids of all ages were given bags filled with candy, nuts, and fruit. The kids gave as well as received. In 1938 and 1939, they collected old or outgrown toys for less fortunate children and bought them to school where they were repaired under the supervision of the shop teacher. On Dec. 22nd, the kids took the toys in a bag, placed it on a doorstep, rang the bell, and ran away.

Quips in the newspaper continued.

• "Prohibition, it might be said, will be a success when a man can have a headache in the morning without being suspected."[187]

• "A senator says Uncle Sam must reduce expenses or increase taxes, so get out the old wallet again."[188]

• "Omar Lattue has a black eye, and his wife has none."[189]

• "… girls who heretofore have restricted their mannish costuming to the beach or the backyard may now come right out in the open and wear trousers to dinner and dance."[190]

Val Kimbrough owned a spacious barber shop on 4th, but it looked more like a mini museum and attracted a lot of repeat visitors. He collected frontier guns, Indian artifacts and weapons, cattle horns, and mounted hunting trophies on the walls. He also caught a variety of local wildlife including tarantulas, Gila monsters, and rattlesnakes, poured alcohol over

Val Kimbrough's museum inside his barber shop. Courtesy Bob Nilson.

them, and displayed them in bottles. Gila monsters and rattlesnakes are both highly poisonous reptiles common in the Benson area.

A dispute arose as to whether the venom of the Arizona rattler was more deadly than that of the Gila monster. To settle the argument, Val caught a live Gila monster and a three and a half foot snake with 7 or 8 rattles. He and his cronies took the animals out to the alley behind the barbershop and put them together in a tub. The snake struck first and "... for 45 minutes thereafter the battle raged fast and furious, both reptiles exchanging thrust with lightning-like rapidity and at the same time sinking their fangs deep into the body of their opponent and hanging on and lunging with all their might. The big lizard showed little reaction to the venom of the rattler but the snake did not escape so easily as the poison secreted by the Gila monster, together with the powerful grip of his jaw which tore into the body of the snake, laid the rattler out at the end. Both

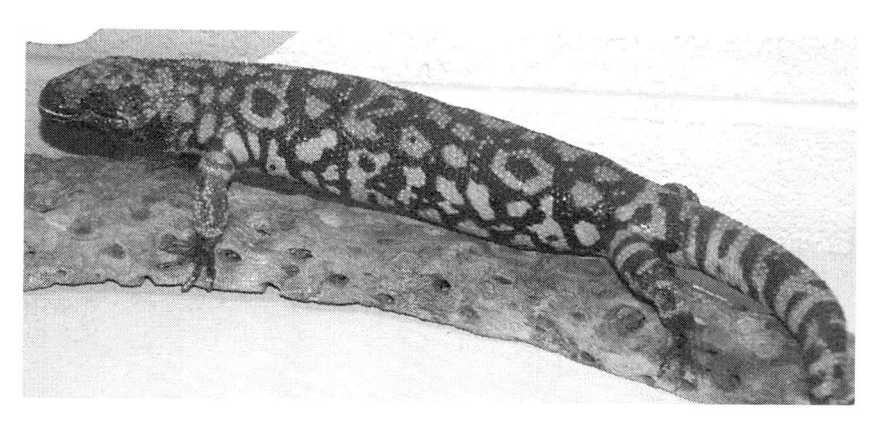

The brightly colored Gila Monster, black with hot pink or orange spots, is a venomous lizard native to the southwestern U.S. and northern Mexico. Typical length for an adult is 20", weight 4 lbs. Courtesy Wikipedia.

reptiles were exhausted when the battle ended but within an hour the Gila monster was as lively as ever and ate his supper with relish, while the rattler was hardly able to move and by the next morning was barely alive."[191]

How dangerous is a Gila Monster to a human? "O.C. Glenn is going around with a bandaged thumb because he tried picking up a Gila monster while out hunting one day last week. The thing swung around and fastened on his thumb and with a mighty swing he (Glenn) shook the thing off but it cut his thumb clear around as neat as if a knife had been used to do the trick."[192] A Gila monster's bite is worse than its venom to humans. A rattlesnake's venom can be fatal.

Despite the Depression, "life goes on" and progress for Benson continued during the second half of the decade.

• The *Tucson Citizen* newspaper was delivered by plane to Benson for the first time in 1937.

• Ads for Tucson stores ran in Benson's *San Pedro Valley News* to draw people to Tucson to shop. The repaved Highway 80 made driving to Tucson easier.

- Air mail left Benson for first time in 1938.
- Mobilgas offered the first credit card in Benson which it advertised as "good throughout the U.S." in 1939.

Relief from the Depression and the Dust Bowl began with the election of President Franklin D. Roosevelt in 1933 and the implementation of his New Deal programs. Benson benefited from the programs. In October of that year, Benson received 1200 pounds of food to be given to families on relief rolls. With the food came recipes for new ways of cooking it. Such food allotments, usually surplus goods, came to Benson once or twice a year. At school, undernourished kids received free lunches, consisting of a hot dish, bread, milk, and fruit.

Roosevelt's main goal, however, was to alleviate the high unemployment rate and boost the country's morale. His public work relief programs created jobs, albeit temporary ones. A participant worked for a given period of time, often six months, on projects that benefited the public. Capping the time period one individual worked increased the number of men who could enroll. For example, the Civilian Conservation Corps' (CCC) maximum enrollment at any one time was 300,000, but in the nine years of its existence, approximately 2.5 million young men participated. They benefited from the temporary income, but also learned marketable job skills.

The CCC came to the San Pedro Valley in 1935 with the establishment of Camp CSC-19-A in St. David. The CCC provided employment for young men between the ages of 18 and 25 while at the same time implementing a natural resource conservation program. Their primary job here was erosion control work on ranches in and around Dragoon, St. David, and Jay Six. For the boys' leisure time, the camp included a baseball diamond, swimming pond, and recreation hall with hardwood floors for dances. Occasionally, for celebrations like July 4th, the camp opened to the public. The CCC dismantled the camp and buildings in 1939 and moved them to Safford.

The Drought Relief Act directly impacted ranchers and farmers. The government bought cattle in counties that were designated emergency areas. In June of 1934, the *San Pedro Valley News* reported that the director of emergency drought relief for Cochise County bought 3,000 head of cattle for $35,000; the following month, July, another $95,000 worth. "The government cattle buying program was a God-send to many farmers [and ranchers], as they could not afford to keep their cattle, and the government paid a better price than they could obtain in local markets."[193] In Cochise County, the government paid $12-20 a head for cattle two years and older, $10-15 for one to two-year-olds, and $4-8 for those under one year. Animals suitable for human consumption were shipped to the Federal Surplus Relief Corporation. They were slaughtered, and the beef distributed to starving families nationwide. Sick or severely famished animals were killed on the range.

While the CCC and the Drought Relief Act targeted ranchers and farmers, all the citizens of Benson benefited from other programs. The short-lived Civil Works Administration (CWA), created jobs but ended only five months after its creation because of criticism that it created jobs but little of permanent value. Benson did benefit during its brief existence. Forty men worked on concrete conduits and drainage outlets for flood waters, curbing, and concrete-lined guttering to combat Bensons' long-standing problems with flood control. They also repaired the town's reservoir tank. As usual with these programs, the town supplied the materials, and the Federal government paid for the labor. Benson could not have afforded the improvements if it had to pay for both.

The Works Progress Administration (WPA) replaced the

CWA and became the principal relief agency of the New Deal. It focused on working with local governments on small construction projects and paid hourly wages based on the prevailing wages of the area. As with the CWA, typically the agency provided the labor and the local government bought the materials.

Benson partnered with the WPA on several projects. In 1934, relief labor repaired the roof on the municipal building and the fire station and cleaned up and weeded the new cemetery. In 1936, Benson received WPA approval for much larger projects. At the grammar school, workers built a concrete tennis court, basketball floor, showers, and a large gutter below the school for flood waters. A project at the high school added a 30 ft. wide by 90 ft. long facility southwest of the main building. It became home to the new Industrial Arts curriculum which taught trades to high school boys and doubled as a storage shed for school buses. The $10,000 project cost the school district $4,000, with the Federal government paying $6,000 in labor wages. The previously-mentioned gas line was a WPA project. A proposed sewer project in 1938 was abandoned when the town estimated its cost at $54,000. Another proposal in 1939 for sidewalks and curbing was likewise abandoned "On account of the lackadaisical attitude of property owners in Benson …"[194] That judgement was a bit harsh, perhaps, considering the city's operating budget for the fiscal year 1934-1935 was $13,3553.50; for 1935-1936, $13,698.00; for 1937-1938, $14, 511; for 1938-1939, $16,025.

Other government programs helped in different ways. 1936 legislation awarded bonus bonds to war veterans. The first bonds for $50 arrived in Benson in June of that year but over time would average up to $500 per vet. The Agricultural Adjustment Act (AAA) of 1938 paid farmers for planting soil-building crops such as alfalfa or clover or using recommended phosphate fertilizers. They had to sign a form of intention to cooperate; 117 farmers in Cochise County did so. Ranchers living on their own ranch could qualify as relief workers and receive wages for feed for their animals. The Social Security Act of 1935 created a system of insurance for the aged, unemployed, and disabled. And, best of all, although the government can't take credit for this one, in the Fall of 1939, the rains came, ending the drought.

New Deal programs got the country back on its feet, but their effectiveness was drawing to a close. "Before Roosevelt's second term was well under way, his domestic program was overshadowed by a new danger little noted by average Americans."[195] That new danger was World War II. War industries would boom, bringing back economic prosperity and the creation of new jobs. Those jobs and the draft resulted in low unemployment.

An editorial statement in the Sept. 1, 1939 issue of the *San Pedro Valley News* hinted at the changes in the wind. "Our little part of the world moves on in spite of the heavy war clouds that are hanging over Europe." But it wasn't long before Bensonites, those "average Americans," faced the consequences of another national conflict.

Depression Prices

1931 prices in Benson compiled from newspaper ads. These prices did not apply to all stores at all times. They were specials meant to draw customers into a specific store as businesses vied with each other for customers. However, the low prices do indicate the effect of the depression.

FOOD

Meat

Bacon	$ .29 lb.
Pork roast	$ .23 lb.
Pork shoulder roast	$ .10 lb.
Pork chops	$ .24 lb.
Pork spareribs	$ .20 lb.
Pot roast	$ .125 lb.
Prime beef pot roast	$ .18 lb.
Hamburger	$ .35 - 2 lbs.
Round steak	$ .27 lb.
Sirloin steak	$ .27 lb.
Prime rib	$ .20 lb.
Rump roast	$ .18 lb.
Veal loin steak	$ .27 lb.
Ham	$ .20 lb.
Swifts premium ham	$ .245 lb.
Wieners	$ .25 lb.
Lard	$ .35 - 2 lbs.
Fresh fish	$ .30 lb.

Staples

Cane sugar:
2 lbs.	$ .14 or .15
5 lbs.	$ .32 or .33
10 lbs.	$ .59

25 lbs.	$1.47 to 1.55
100 lbs.	$5.69
Flour:	
5 lbs.	$ .21
10 lbs.	$ .36
24 lbs.	$ .79
48 lbs.	$1.50
Cake flour	$ .37 pkg.
Bread	$ .10 loaf
Pasta:	
Macaroni	$ .25 - 4 pkgs.
Spaghetti	$ .25 - 4 pkgs.
Noodles	$ .25 - 4 pkgs.
Pinto beans	$ .05 lb.
Potatoes:	
individual	$ .03 lb.
10 lbs.	$ .18 to .26
Rice	$ .09 lb.

Diary

Eggs	$ .19 or .20
Milk*	$ .33 - 4 tall cans
Milk*	$ .33 - 8 small cans
Wisconsin cheese	$ .24 lb.
Cream cheese	$ .24 lb.

*Two dairies in town, Coons and Ruckers, delivered fresh milk twice daily.

Vegetables

Beets	$ .05 - 2 bunches
Cabbage	$ .02 lb.
Carrots	$ .05 - 2 bunches
Lettuce	$ .07
Onions	$ .05 - 2 bunches

Fruit

Apples	$ .21 - 3 lbs.
Bananas	$ .26 lb.
Barlett pears	$ .15 tin
Del Monte peaches	$ .22 can
Dole pineapple	$ .26
Grapefruit	$ .11 to .14 for 6
Lemons	$ .15 dozen
Oranges	$ .29 dozen
Plums	$ .05 or .06 lb.
Tomatoes	$ .05 to .08 lb.
Watermelon	$ .02 lb.

Miscellaneous

Aunt Jemima pancake flour	$ .33 large
Best Foods bread and butter pickles	$ .18 - 15 oz. jar
Campbells soup	$ .10 or 3 for $.27
Catchup	$ .15 bottle
Corn flakes	$ .15 for 2
English walnuts	$ .27 lb.
Jello	$ .25 for 3
Lipton tea	$ .09 or 3 for .25
Maxwell House coffee	$ .38 lb.
MSB coffee	$ .40 lb.
Mazola oil	$ .29 pint/.54 quart
Raisins	$ .10 - 1 lb. bag
Large ripe olives	$ .16 - 9 oz.
Spanish stuffed olives	$ .15 - 3 oz.
Van de Camps pork and beans	$ .05 - 6 oz. can

Thanksgiving Specials

Dressed turkey	$ .25 lb.
Pork roast	$ .20 lb.
Cranberries	$ .17 lb.
Fresh pumpkin pie	$ .25 each

Benson's Ride through History: 1880 - 1945

CLOTHING

Boys' dress shirts	$ .75
Men's dress shirts	$1.49
Men's dress pants	$3.98
Men's work pants	$ .39
Men's rayon shirts	$ .59
Men's rayon shorts	$ .59
Men's shoes	$1.35 - 2.95
Leather palmed gloves	$ .19
Men's socks	$ .10 -.19
Men's dress socks	$ .25
Men's ties	$ .10 - .69
Men's wool suits	$24.95
Ladies dresses	$10.00 - 14.50
Ladies house dresses	$ .79 - .98
Ladies silk blouses	$2.98
Ladies hose	$ .29
Ladies silk hose	$ .98
Ladies silk bras	$ .98
Ladies hats	$1.39
Ladies suits	$3.95
Ladies jackets	$4.95
Ladies shoes	$2.95
Children's coveralls	$ .89
Children's sweaters	$ .98
Children's shoes	$ .89 and up

TOOLS

Hammer	$1.00
Saw	$2.25
Hack saw	$ .55
Compass saw	$ .90
Plane	$1.50, $3.75
Screw driver	$ .25
Files	$ .15

Hand axes	$1.75
Bench screws	$1.50
Tin snips	$1.25
Rubber hose	$ .12 ft.
Sprinklers	$1.00
Hoes	$1.25
Shovels	$1.50
Trowels	$ .40
Nozzles	$ .65
Sprinkling cans	$1.25
Rakes	$1.45
Flower seeds	$ .10 pkg.
Vegetable seeds	$ .10 pkg.

HOUSEHOLD ITEMS

Dish soap	$ .37 - 2 lb. 8 oz. pkg.
Ivory soap flakes	$ .15 - 2 small pkgs.
Sunbright cleanser	$ .10 for 2
Toilet paper:	
Ambassador roll	$ .07
Scott roll	$ .10
Brooms	$ .34
Feather pillow	$ .79 - 1.00
Baby blankets	$ .23, .49, .69
Cotton blankets	$ .79 - 1.00
Comforters	$1.98
Pillow cases	$ .15
Fabric	$ .15 yd.

Chapter 11

Hang on, Cowboy

In 1883, William Frederick Cody, better known as Buffalo Bill, started his Buffalo Bill's Wild West. The show[196] began with a parade on horseback with performers dressed in colorful costumes. During the main events, performers re-enacted trips on the Pony Express, Indian attacks on wagon trains, and stagecoach robberies. The show included staged races and demonstrations of feats of skill such as sharpshooting by celebrities Annie Oakley and her husband Frank Butler. "The finale was typically a portrayal of an Indian attack on a settler's cabin. Cody would ride in with an entourage of cowboys to defend the settler and his family."[197]

Buffalo Bill's Wild West's prestige in both the United States and Europe birthed the concept of "rodeo" which became popular throughout the West. Rodeo events were linked to ranch activities. They allowed cowboys a way to exhibit their skills in friendly competition while offering a venue for exciting entertainment at a time when movies and radio were in their infancy and television still in the future. Tucson began its rodeo in 1924 and later promoted it as "providing entertainment to thousands of winter visitors." The rodeo became a symbol of status for a western cattle town.

Rodeos drew crowds from far and near. Bensonites traveled to other towns to attend rodeos, and local cowboys competed in events. Benson businessmen talked about a rodeo as a way to bring people to Benson to help boost the town's economy. In 1934, Pete Haverty, Val Kimbrough, Page Lee, Kearney Gardner, and W.A. Evans formed a committee to plan Benson's first rodeo which they named the San Pedro Valley Rodeo. The days of flying ropes and jingling spurs had arrived in Benson.

The committee didn't skimp on the "Really Big Show" as the newspaper shouted in a large headline. The two-day rodeo, scheduled for Labor Day weekend, August 18 and 19, featured a calf-roping contest, steer riding, horse and novelty cow races by

Ernest Browning demonstrating his calf-roping skills during the 1935 rodeo. Cars formed a ring around the open field to serve as a fence. Courtesy Ed Lee.

Benson businessmen, team tying, and bronco riding with all events to be announced on the loud-speaker.

The rodeo included more than arena events. The town pitched in to make it a success. The $.50 admission fee, children under 12 free, included a free barbeque. Local ranchers donated the beef and volunteers cooked it. The rodeo opened with a colorful parade down Main Street with the cowboys dressed in their finest. A dance Saturday night in the Benson Auditorium cost an additional $.50. The popular Skyline club closed that night "in order that everyone may attend the rodeo dance." Hoping to cash in on the expected crowds, businesses took out ads in the newspaper hawking rodeo supplies and services available for visitors.

Page's Palace became the headquarters for the rodeo where cowboys picked up their cash prizes and celebrated with friends. Courtesy Ed Lee.

The committee advertised in Benson, Tucson, and other city newspapers, but Page Lee also traveled to nearby towns and left signs advertising the rodeo at businesses. His bar, Page Lee's Pool Hall, later renamed Page's Palace, was headquarters for the rodeo, where the cowboys came to pick up their cash prizes and celebrate with friends. He also sponsored boxing bouts, no doubt with a little betting on the side. So the bar was packed, and Page kept eight to ten bartenders on duty for the weekend.

Looking toward the rear of Page's Palace on a non-rodeo day. Courtesy Ed Lee.

The first rodeo arena was about two miles out of town, north on Ocotillo Road, near where KOA would later build a campground. The ground was level, well-drained with shade and water, and provided a place to feed the stock. Corrals and chutes were built, but no fence. Cars parked in a ring served as the fence, with an opening on the far end to get the animals in and out for each event.

All the effort paid off. 2,000 people attended the rodeo, well over double Benson's population at the time. So began an annual event which grew over the years. Virgil Haverty, one of the top rodeo champions in the Southwest during the early 1940s, called the rodeo "the biggest holiday in Benson every year." And while the cowboys took their events seriously, novelty races such as the businessmen's steer or cow riding race added fun and laughs. "I remember Harold Holcomb," said Haverty, "who was a businessman here, one of the owners of K&H Grocery store, he got in it. He was a small, bald-headed guy. They put him on a big cow and let it out. He rode her, but he didn't get off. He went clear down and out of the arena. Finally the cowboys held him up down at the bottom end and got him off. He said they told him how to get on but no one told him how to get off. He just rode it till they stopped her and took him off."[198] The rodeo was always held on Labor Day weekend, just before the start of school.

In 1936, C.S. Rucker added a fence to the rodeo grounds. Except for rodeo weekend, he used the area as pasture for cows and young stock. Rucker owned the Willow Grove Dairy on the north edge of town near the arena. Unfortunately, two years later while repairing a small corral, he was gored to death by his Guernsey bull. It's believed the accident occurred as he led the bull by a chain to take him to water.

Cattle ranching continued to be a leading industry in the San Pedro Valley, so the San Pedro Valley Rodeo was not only popular but also an apt activity to celebrate its ranching status. In 1938, Cochise County ranked 11th among the 50 leading counties in the number of cattle, with Willcox becoming the major cattle shipping center. A problem arose in 1937, as the newspaper reported in its August 6th edition that "It looked for a while as if Benson's annual Labor Day rodeo would fall by the wayside." Although not specifically identified in the newspaper article, a problem apparently arose among the rodeo committee members. Page Lee, who had been on the rodeo committee from the start, took over sponsorship of the rodeo with his friend G.W. (Booser) Page of Willcox and saved the rodeo. They would continue as the rodeo organizers for many years to come, with the support and help of the town.

The 1937 rodeo featured calf roping, bull riding, team tying, bulldogging, wild cow milking, a rope horse race, a pony express race, and free-for-all races. The dance took place as usual on Saturday night, and the free barbeque continued, but prices rose to $.75 for adults and $.25 for children under 12. The sponsors also added concession stands selling beer and soft drinks, sandwiches, and ice cream.

Hype for the 1939 rodeo, scheduled for September 3rd and 4th, began in mid-July with a whisker growing contest. Men who signed up for the contest could not shave until September 5th or would be fined $2.50. They also had to "go Western" and wear a big hat and cowboy handkerchief or cowboy boots and Levis and a loud cowboy shirt. Fifty-one men signed up to compete for the prizes for best whiskers.

1941 Costs for "Rodeo Clothes" in Benson

Levis	$1.95
10 gallon hat	$1.95
Stetson	$7.50 and up
Bandanas	$0.35
Gabardine shirts	$3.95 and up
Belts	$1.00 and up
Frontier pants	$3.75 and up
Boots	$6.45

1939 also brought the first rodeo accident. "Jack Finley of the Four F Ranch caused much concern when the steer he roped by the waistline instead of the neck resented such treatment and dragged the horse down. The horse landed on Jack, and before the dust had cleared away the ambulance had Jack inside and was headed for Tucson. Almost everybody thot (thought) he was dead but Jack rose to a sitting position and that fear was allayed." He received the Hard Luck Cowboy prize. "Asked if would need any special treatment because of the fall, he replied, "Yeah, I'll have to take a bath."[199]

The only tragic accident would not occur until 1947. For the horse races, the arena had a gate just past the finish line. The horses would gallop full speed to the finish line and continue through the gate before slowing down. Unfortunately for Armado Sotilo from the Bar AA Ranch in Nogales, someone forgot to open the gate during his race. "The mishap occurred as a matched race took place when the barbed wire gates were closed in the middle of the race. Sotilo's horse hit the barbed wire fence and fell on him. He suffered a severe concussion, a punctured right eye, bruises and both arms broken." Sotilo died from the injuries several days later.[200]

The 1940s started well for the rodeo. The newspaper boasted of the "largest crowds ever at Labor Day Rodeo" and editorialized the feelings of the town in the statement, "Surely they'll (Page and Booser) schedule another for it has become traditional with Benson and it cannot be let pass away." Concern for the rodeo probably arose from the clouds of war hanging over the future.

The rodeo took place as usual in 1942. The August 7th edition of the *San Pedro Valley News* reported, "The San Pedro Valley Labor Day Rodeo will go on just the same this year although many of the young performers will be away in the

Although not clearly visible , cars are parked side-by-side on the far left of the photo past the crowd. They form part of the ring around the arena. The car visible through the crowd, also part of the ring, indicates the size of the arena. Courtesy Bob Nilson.

armed forces. The time may be a little slower on some events but yet men who have been taking part in rodeos for years will be here to out on one of the best shows Benson has ever had."

But the following year, 1943, the August 20th headlines in the *San Pedro Valley News* announced, "No Rodeo This Year." In the article, promoter Page Lee said, "We have decided not to have our rodeo this year for we can't find a room in town. So we can't invite two or three thousand people here and not feed them nor have rooms for them." The gas, food, and lodging shortages caused by the war had taken their toll.

Part of the housing shortage was due to two of the travel courts being rented out on a long-term basis. In August 1942, "Lyndon Hargrave signed a lease for his camp, The Oasis, for the duration of the war to a group of Negro doctors' wives. The doctors are stationed at Fort Huachuca." A point was made in the article that the wives were setting up temporary homes for their husbands and would not be bringing their children.[201]

A few months later, an article in the October 9th edition of the newspaper announced that the Kings Rest Court had also been leased to "Colored Officers and Their Wives ... So there will be no problem with their children going to school in Arizona, these people have only their very small children with them. ... All of the women who are living here are well-read and many of them have college educations. ... There will be no race problem for these people want to have a home here and trade here but will stay to themselves just as the colored people are doing who

Page's Palace during the 1944 rodeo. The composition of the crowd had changed partially because many of the young men had gone to fight the war. The young boy in the photo is Ed Lee, Page Lee's son. Courtesy Ed Lee.

have rented The Oasis." The families stayed for two years, leaving in May 1944.

The rodeo resumed in 1944, although still affected by the war shortages. "True, there were more local people present, more from Willcox and Cochise County and less from Tucson and distant places due to the gasoline shortage, but the crowd was nearly equal to that of former years."[202] Page tried to combat the gas problem by promising gas rationing stamps for people to get home if they'd come to the rodeo, but he never gave any out. He didn't have to; no one asked for them. The promoters also added a dance on Sunday night, in addition to the usual Saturday night dance, with the Troubadours playing both nights.

Page Lee and Booser Page dedicated the 1945 rodeo, Benson's 12th, to returning vets. The end of the war and the lifting of gas rationing boosted attendance by allowing people to travel from farther away. The sponsors even provided a bus to run between downtown Benson and the rodeo grounds. The San Pedro Valley Rodeo was back on solid ground.

Chapter 12

The 1940s: Clouds of War

The Prewar Years

With the official end of the Depression in 1939 and the rains having ended the drought, Bensonites relaxed a bit and focused on local issues. They bought their license plates in January when the state representative came to town and maybe splurged on new Firestone tires for the car for $5.78-$9.68, depending on the tire size. The town bought a new set of tires for its fire truck in June of 1941. The original tires, purchased in 1929, had lasted

4th Street and San Pedro. Gas stations lined 4th to handle the increase in traffic flowing through Benson. Courtesy Bob Nilson.

13 years: they only had 245 miles on them. As 'motoring' became more popular, so did the accidents. The *San Pedro Valley News* ran articles on safety tips. "If every driver would at all times stay on his own side of the road a lot of bad accidents would be avoided. Sideswiping and collisions would be practically unknown."[203] Some things don't change.

With money more plentiful and travelers bringing business into town, Benson enjoyed a period of growth. More gas stations and motels opened. A new "rest court", The Arledon, now competed with the Kings Rest Court, Camp Benson, the Oasis Court, and the O.K.

Typical layout of "rest courts." This court had some units with "door-less" garages for parking cars. Courtesy Bob Nilson.

The city constructed a new municipal building with a large meeting room, a garage for the fire truck with a sleeping room for the custodian who looked after the truck, restrooms, and closets. The Community Presbyterian Church was remodeled and stained glass windows added. As with many construction jobs, the completion date was uncertain. "All the children who attend the Benson Community Church Sunday School will be listening for the church bell to ring Sunday morning. If it rings, Sunday school will be held in the new building, if it does not ring the children will again go to the Benson Theatre where Sunday school has been held all summer."[204]

Businesses blossomed. The Horseshoe, Grill, and Elite cafes redecorated. "Do you know they serve nearly 400 cups of coffee a day at the Horseshoe Café? That's a lot of coffee!!!"[205] The K&H, Community Cash, Hi Wo's, and Quihuiz stores delivered groceries several times a day. The era of trading stamps had arrived. The Community Cash Store dispersed "Blue" stamps with food purchases, and Raleigh cigarettes packs included coupons redeemable for items such as gilt-edged playing cards, roller skates, a bridge table and chairs, cookbooks, and a catalogue full of other items.

Recreation possibilities abounded with a golf course, an indoor rifle range, a skating rink, and on school grounds, a tennis court, football field, baseball diamond, and outdoor track. To encourage women to start bowling, the new bowling alley

The popular Troubadours played at many Benson dances.
Courtesy Ed Ellsworth.

offered free bowling to the ladies on Monday and Tuesday from 9 a.m. till noon. Risners Carnival came to town in 1940 and the Russell Brothers Circus in 1941. In the evenings, adults listened to the popular Troubadours or other bands playing dance music at the White Spot, the Benson Auditorium, or the Skyline Club. Admission to dances generally cost $.50. And, of course, there were the movies.

Movies generally played for only one day, but there were always exceptions. Tickets for the movie *Gone with the Wind* sold out in advance for its first showing in Benson in 1940. When the movie returned in August 1941, it commanded two showings with record crowds at both and record prices for tickets: matinee $.40 for adults / $.25 for children. The evening show was $.55 for either.

In the Fall of 1940, construction began on a new theatre on 4th Street between the Grill Café and Page's Palace. Directions in Benson were given as "between, next to, near, on the corner of," etc. The reason for that is sometimes misunderstood, as in "By 1931, Hi Wo's store was so well-known in Benson that the proprietor of a shoe shop advertised no street address, simply 'Near Hi Wo's'."[206] While Hi Wo's certainly was well-known, the real reason the ad did not include a street address was because street numbers did not exist in Benson until the late 1960s. People identified locations by referencing landmarks.

The new Benson Theatre seated approximately 450. A lighted marque out front announced the next movie, and a new feature in the newspaper, a movie guide, listed the movies for the upcoming week. The cost of equipment at $10,000 easily surpassed the $6,000 cost of the building. Besides the big screen, the theatre featured a 20-foot deep stage for live performances with a basement and a loft to permit stage scenery to be lifted out of the audience's sight. Unfortunately, to make room for the building, a giant old cottonwood tree, 25' x 140', had to be removed. The tin building on 5th Street, the auditorium, that used to serve as the movie house continued to be used for dances and skating. It was dismantled in 1944; wood from the interior was reused for building the Quarter Horse Motel.

One amusement was taken away during the decade. As mentioned earlier, thieves broke into the Lee's Pool Hall and opened the slot machines for cash they may contain. It was not unusual for a restaurant, bar, or other place of entertainment to have gambling machines. The Horseshoe Café was in the process of converting the second story into a gambling casino in the early 1940s.

"Arizona has a long history with gaming, owing to its status as a one-time frontier state. The state's political attitude grew

The Horseshoe Cafe and Bakery on 4th Street has been a popular Benson restaurant for decades.

The inside of the Horseshoe Cafe with its trademark Neon horseshoe on the ceiling. Courtesy Patty Colombo.

more staunchly conservative over the years, so that by the mid-20th century, all forms of gambling were illegal."[207] Indian casinos on tribal lands were exempted. Cochise County began enforcing state law and cracking down on the operation of all slot machines, marble machines, and similar devices. Any devices found would be confiscated and the owner would face a fine, imprisonment, or both.

Thus, the casino in the Horseshoe was never finished or opened. Mabel Williams lived there, instead, after her husband died. The slot machines were still there but not operational. Mabel was an alcoholic involved in AA. A neighbor called the police one night and said Mabel was running a gambling hall upstairs. The police broke into the upstairs and found an AA meeting going on. In fact, they broke in right in the middle of the Lord's Prayer so were quite embarrassed.

Bensonites took in stride the periodic floods that have plagued the town since its beginning. The June rains of 1940 broke a 60 year record, which made the cattlemen happy as June was usually the driest month of the year. In July, the river rose 15 feet from heavy rains, and a month later a new dike in the river broke, no longer able to hold back the accumulation of water. What wasn't usual were the shock waves from the Imperial Valley earthquake on May 18, 1940. "Virgil Roberts was on duty at the agricultural inspection station sitting in a straight back chair with his feet on his desk waiting for cars to come by when all of a sudden the lights began to swing back and forth and his chair to slide. He got up and rushed over to The Oasis Camp and said to Mrs. Newton, 'Am I drunk or just what is going on anyway?'"[208]

The completion of Highways 80 and 86 in the late 1930s had put Benson once more on the map as a travel town. However, the awkward transition from one highway to another caused considerable problems. Trucks coming into town on Highway 86 still lost their brakes when coming downhill into

A new interchange solved the transition problem between Highways 80 and 86 by creating an underpass: trains traveled on top, cars on Highway 86 passed underneath. Courtesy Bob Nilson.

Benson or picked up speed during the descent and came through the business district too fast. Some wrecked on the east end of town because they were unable to negotiate the bend in the road.

To remedy the situation, construction began in 1940 on an interchange and a new underpass to permit a smoother convergence between the two highways. The newspaper touted it as an "ultra-modern design" claiming it was the first structure in Arizona to combine separation of both highway traffic and the railroad. Trains traveled on the four tracks on top of the bridge while vehicles on Highway 86 passed under the bridge. A traffic circle permitted transition between the highways. When the underpass opened in January of 1942, the old highway approach to the city was fenced off. The project, which cost the state $212,129.86, marked a new beginning in Benson's history.

Whether travelers took the new transcontinental Highway 80 or its shortcut Highway 86, they were routed through Benson. The town would prosper from the heavy flow of traffic and grow. The 1940 census listed Benson's population at 970; by 1947, the newspaper claimed 1200. World War II, however, postponed the anticipated benefits as wartime shortages and rationing of tires, fuel, and oil restricted recreational travel.

War broke out in Europe in 1939. Most Americans, Bensonites included, paid little attention at first to the conflict "over there." As 1940 advanced toward 1942, however, the conflict seemed to be creeping its way across the ocean as the United States government began wartime preparations under the umbrella of National Defense.

The Selective Training and Service Act of 1940 put the draft into effect and imposed a quota per state for one year of army training. Arizona met its first quota in November of 1940 with 147 volunteers. Registration soon became mandatory as the

Selective Service imposed new quotas every few months. Farmers were the first to feel the labor shortages caused by the rearmament program when migrant workers were "deflected into work in connection with the defense program. ... Who kept the Okies from keeping their date in the harvest field? Why Herr Hitler, of course."[209]

Traffic increased to a heavy volume on the railroads transporting workers to various defense projects such as the installation of an all-cable transcontinental telephone line. Begun during the summer of 1941, the telephone line was "designed to meet any demands that may arise for communication between centers of industry, railheads, troop concentration points, and defense centers from coast to coast."[210]

To pay for all this activity, the government needed money. In May of 1941, the National Defense Fund began selling bonds and stamps. Raising taxes was another source of income. In March of 1941, the Apache Powder Company gave bonus checks to employees for their "cooperation and loyal support." However, the company also warned that the bonuses were "not to be considered as an established practice because of increasing taxation."[211] In 1936, the company paid $97,646.61 in taxes. By 1940, that amount rose to $198,946.31, an increase of over 100 percent in four years.

On October 3, 1941, more than a year before the U.S. entered the war, the *San Pedro Valley News* ran a huge ad about conserving rubber, considered to be a raw material vital to national defense. The great fear was that the U.S. might be cut off from its suppliers. Car owners were asked to help conserve rubber by keeping wheels aligned and tires properly inflated and rotated, by not speeding and by avoiding quick starts and sudden stops.

Other hints about impending involvement in the war included news of ships being built, conversion of plants to defense work, and the training of workers in such plants. Locally, Fort Huachuca expanded with the addition of approximately 4500 trainees and workers. While the Army continued the draft, it also recruited volunteers in ads such as "Help Wanted: Male 18-25, Army training: welding, aviation mechanics, sheet metal, aerial photography, radio."[212]

The Navy, too, pushed for enlistments. One sailor from Benson, Louis Robinson, wrote home in July of 1940 about his participation in a competition between Navy ships. His letter was summarized in the newspaper to share news of him. "Recently he and his pal Dully Mathes won second place in the fleet rifle matches which placed their ship, the USS Arizona, in second place. This pleased the captain so that he gave the boys on the rifle team a turkey dinner which, according to Louis, was 'tops.' The boys were also each given a $5 prize and will receive expert riflemen awards. Louis writes about coming back to the United States, but he says the fleet has no idea how much longer it will be stationed in Hawaii. 'I do hope it will be soon.' Louie is at Pearl Harbor."[213] Louis's hope was realized when the ship returned to the mainland for an overhaul in the fall of 1940 and he was allowed to go "on liberty." The USS Arizona, with Louis on board, returned to Pearl Harbor in February 1941, but it would never come home again.

The War Years

The Japanese dropped their bombs on Pearl Harbor on Sunday, December 7, 1941. The bombs sank the USS Arizona, entombing 1177 of the 1400 sailors on board. The next day President Roosevelt asked Congress to declare war on Japan.

Three days later, December 11th, Germany and Italy, as allies of Japan, declared war on United States and the U.S. reciprocated. The country would no longer be watching the war from the sidelines.

**Bombing of the USS Arizona on December 7, 1941.
Courtesy National Archives and Records Administration.**

Perhaps because the attack occurred on a Sunday and the *San Pedro Valley News* came out on Fridays, the newspaper did not mention the assault on Pearl Harbor. Five days later, other media and word-of-mouth had already spread the news. The newspaper did cover the declaration of war against Germany and Italy in its December 12th edition in a relatively short article; most of it the President's address to Congress. "The long known and long expected has thus taken place. The forces endeavoring to enslave the entire world are now moving toward this hemisphere."[214]

Although the government had been stepping up its military

The burnt-out wreck of the USS Arizona as it sank to its watery grave. Courtesy U.S. Navy.

defenses for a couple of years, entry into the war was a rude awakening for many Americans who thought of it as a European war. Changes came quickly. In the same issue that carried news of the declaration of war, the newspaper informed its readers that they would no longer be reporting the weather. "In the interests of national defense, publication of temperatures has been discontinued on order of the War and Navy Departments."

As its first response to the war, Benson formed a home defense committee and educated its citizens about what to do if there's an air raid: stay home, get out of street, put out lights, stay away from windows, keep quiet, don't believe wild rumors, keep radios turned on, and, if bombs fell, lie down whether at home or outside. An editorial in January, however, criticized the committee's work saying that while it had set up guidelines for acting during or after an event, it failed to set up a warning system to signal an impending air raid. The committee added alert signals.

Housewives busied themselves making black out curtains from old materials around the house because not only was new material expensive, but it was difficult to get. The looms and machinery that produced yardage had been commandeered for military needs. By February, Arizonans practiced blackouts statewide: no operating cars, stay home and off the streets, or pay a severe penalty if non-compliant. In May, Benson had a practice air raid. Planes flew over and dropped pasteboard plaques representing four different kinds of bombs. Anyone finding a "bomb" had to notify the air raid warden who would give further instructions.

Changes began immediately. Less than a month after the declaration of war, rationing of tires began. Restrictions increased through the year 1942, all with the idea of conserving rubber, a critical material in defense work. To get a new tire, an owner had to prove to the War Price & Rationing Office in Benson that it did not become unusable through abuse or neglect. To conserve rubber, a "war speed" of 40 mph began in July, but was reduced to 35 mph by October. The war speed applied to busses and trucks as well as cars and was strictly enforced. Many a driver paid a $25.00 fine or ended up in jail for excessive speed. A school bus used for any purpose other than transferring teachers and pupils to and from classes was not even eligible for new tires.

The government placed a special revenue tax on autos of $5.00 a year. The driver bought a yearly stamp which he carried with him on a card. By the end of 1942, gas rationing also went into effect, both gas for cars and "non-highway" gas for washing machines, stationary machines, lamps, cleaning, etc. By the beginning of 1943, tires had to be inspected to assure gas and tires in the future. Meanwhile, the government set ceilings on prices for used tires and tubes to stop unscrupulous dealers from using the rubber shortage to hike prices.

The rationing of tires and gas affected not only the traveler but would change the lifestyle of Benson shoppers. In January 1942, the Community Cash Store, the K&H Store, Hi Wo's, and the Quihuiz grocery restricted deliveries to twice a day because of the rationing on tires and tubes. By May, merchants reduced deliveries to once a day per family. By 1943, stores didn't deliver at all. As the K&H ad in the March 5, 1943 edition of the newspaper pointed out, "No deliveries Because You Have To Have Your Ration Book Anyway."

K&H, Community Cash, Hi Wo's, and the Fair Store also cut their hours and closed at 6:30 p.m., in cooperation with the defense program. The Community Cash Store permanently closed its doors in late 1942 after a decade of service, when the owners went into the Army. They planned to reopen "after this is all over," but never did. J.P. Plough bought the store in September 1944 and turned it into Plough's Grocery & Market.

First tires, then sugar. Sugar rationing began in May 1942, a pound per person each two weeks. For sugar, and eventually other food commodities, people were issued ration books with stamps redeemable at a merchant's. The process of issuing ration books was a huge undertaking, fraught with complications. Benson Grammar School closed on May 4, 1942, for one day to issue the first ration books. Although one member of the family could apply for the entire family, a separate application had to be filed for each person. Teachers, acting as registrars, processed about five applications per hour.

Rationing amounts and products would change as the war progressed and new books would be issued. For example, to save manpower in the packaging and handling of sugar, the allotment changed in March of 1943 to five pounds each 11 weeks, slightly less per person than before, but reverted back in June 1944 when the allotment changed again to five pounds each 10 weeks. The issuance of new books invalidated any stamps left-over from the old book. What if someone lost a book? Consumers had to wait two months after the date of application to receive a replacement for a lost ration book.

Once merchants collected stamps, they were supposed to affix their code numbers on the stamp with a rubber stamp. The ever-tightening ban on the use of rubber, however, even in minor consumer articles, meant they could not replace worn rubber stamps. Eventually, they were allowed to print their code number on the stamps in ink.

As the war progressed and the list of rationed items grew, people swapped stamps to obtain more of a needed product. Coffee made the list in November 1942. Mormons in St. David and Pomerene did not drink coffee but did can much of the produce grown on their farms. They often traded with their coffee drinking neighbors to obtain more sugar for their canning. Then came the rationing of meat: fresh, frozen, cured, smoked, and canned. Next came canned food, in general, including edible fats and oils, butter, cheese, fruits and vegetables, and shoes.

Merchants had their own headaches trying to implement the rules. During the first week of sugar rationing, "The cafes the first of the week were trying various means of rationing the sugar and no two are carrying out the same program."[215] Grocers were also rationed by the amount of sugar they could stock. Merchants had as much trouble as consumers obtaining other food. "Because he could get no meat, Dick Hieber closed his café all day last Saturday."[216] In an ad, the K&H Store pleaded for the return of Coca Cola bottles. "They Tell Us No Bottles! No Cokes!"[217] Local dairies also wanted their milk bottles back. Laura's Café, open less than a year, closed in 1945 "for lack of rationing points necessary to feed the large volume of business."[218] Don's Coffee Shop opened in the same location two weeks later.

The availability of canned fruits and vegetables was cut 50% by March 1943. To combat this ever-dwindling supply of food, people planted more and more "victory gardens," individual or community, to raise their own food. In 1943, Benson High School added a class in vegetable gardening to its curriculum, and the girls started a co-op victory garden at school. "By 1945, an estimated 20 million victory gardens produced approximately 40 percent of America's vegetables."[219] Many items were not rationed but were in short supply, such as soap and alcohol. The Kellogg Company, on the other hand, advertised their "plentiful" supply of cereals as non-rationed food.

Rationing grew worse in the waning days of the war. The push continued for people to plant victory gardens to compensate for the lack of commercially grown produce. Meat allotments went from two and a half pounds per person per week in 1943 to a half-pound per person per week in 1945. In response to that cut, Myer Stolaroff, President of the Benson Chamber of Commerce, wrote in a letter to Senator Carl Hayden: "Is it the duty of the governing agencies to see that the people obey the law or are they trying to force the people to break them ... when they pass a regulation that any inmate of an insane asylum could see that it is stupid."[220]

Uncle Sam needed a multitude of materials for the war, many of them in short supply or difficult to import from other countries, so why not re-use old materials? "Recycling was born with the government's encouragement."[221] Metal from tin cans made shells for the 75-mm Howitzer. Waste cooking fats made glycerin for explosives.

Recycling began almost immediately. When the call came in 1941 to save waste paper, the Boy Scouts took over the task. They went from house to house and collected about a ton. During a salvage drive for rubber in July 1942, Benson collected 68,229 pounds of rubber. August 1942 brought the first National Junk Drive. The American Legion Auxiliary in Willcox collected scrap iron and steel, scrap rubber, collapsible tin tubes, waste cooking fats, and old manila rope and burlap that could be recycled for military use. The K&H Store bought waste oil at $.04 a pound for the Kitchen Fats Salvage Campaign.

A second junk drive in October met with such a "lousy" response that it prompted an editorial in the October 23rd edition lambasting Bensonites for being lazy. That put a little fire into their souls. The next edition reported that volunteers rounded up 30 tons of scrap in one day. "So enthusiastic did the firemen become Sunday when they were gathering junk from all over Benson that they took a woman's stove and had to return it." The various drives certainly provided a place for Bensonites to dispose of used and unneeded materials, but they still held their annual clean up campaigns to spruce up homes and businesses by repairing, painting, weeding, and picking up garbage.

Benson's most important contributions, of course, were the young men who marched off to fight. From the day *The San Pedro Valley News* ran its article on the declaration of war, it voiced its support by adding the slogan "Stand Firm America" to its heading. The newspaper devoted many column inches throughout the war to "the boys" sent to fight. Issue after issue contained reports of who entered the service, where they were stationed, who was on furlough and where, who received promotions, who was discharged, their photographs and, unfortunately, who was killed, missing, or a POW. The editor published letters sent by servicemen to share their news with the entire town. He also sent copies of the newspaper free to any serviceman who requested it, thus allowing the soldiers and sailors to learn news not only about home but also about their friends in the service from the published letters.

Perhaps the most poignant letter came from Louis Robinson, the sailor mentioned earlier who was stationed on the USS Arizona in Pearl Harbor at the time of the Japanese attack. "Well, aside from a little swim in the harbor," he wrote, "and my ears ringing for a couple of days, I am perfectly O.K. I lost everything I had except my shoes and pants which was all I had left after the battle ... God, how I long for a pretty girl and an Arizona moon. Sure, I look at this Hawaiian moon out here, but it's when I am on watch and looking for those damn Japs to come back. Yes, now we have to lick every single one of the yellow *** before we can get back to a normal life again. For instance, I kissed a girl yesterday, she had one eye closed (bless her heart) the other looking up in the sky for enemy airplanes and both ears open, listening for an air raid warning siren. Now how the devil is a guy going to enjoy life until we do lick those Japs? I ask you."[222]

Bensonites supported the servicemen through fund-raisers for the USO and Red Cross; by mailing cards and gifts to servicemen, particularly at Christmas time; through book drives for soldiers in camps, training and rec centers, ships, and barracks; and especially by buying war bonds and stamps. There were seven war bond drives or loans in all, the last started just before the end of the war. The name of the seventh drive, therefore, changed to Victory Loan Bonds, rather than War Loan

Bonds. The push to buy was constant. In the early days of the war, local merchants participated in a nationwide movement of suspending sales for 15 minutes and devoting this period to the sale of war stamps and bonds exclusively. Local schools held competitions to sell stamps. Stamps usually cost 10 cents each and could be accumulated toward the purchase of a bond. The newspaper ran slogans such as "Invest 10% of what you earn in war bonds" or this advice when listing the names of servicemen, "The above list of names represents to this neighborhood nearly seven hundred reasons why War Bonds should be of concern and we at home should Pitch In To Win." Bonds kept the war wheels grinding. "More than 85 million Americans - half the population - purchased bonds totaling $185.7 billion."[223]

As human loss from the war mounted, the military needed to expand its resources beyond male enlistments. A newspaper article in the February 26th, 1943 edition talked about dogs being trained for Army duty because "One dog and one man equal at least half a dozen sentries and release that manpower for actual combat." The Army and Navy also began actively recruiting women through advertising. 1943 Navy campaigns pushed women to enlist in the WAVES to "release a sailor to man our ships and fly our planes."

At the beginning of the war, Benson High School placed curriculum emphasis on vocational, science, and math subjects to prepare the boys for military service and offered a defense class in metal work for men. By 1943, the high school also offered elementary electricity and refresher math classes with books furnished by the government, the same books used by the Army and Navy for transition into service. A big difference was that these courses were now open to females.

The number of men in service created difficulties for businesses because it depleted the work force. The K&H Store, for example, lost two employees and could not replace them. Before the war, customers went to the counter, placed their order, and clerks fetched the items for them. This was no longer possible with a shortage of help. So the store was rearranged to allow customers access to the stock. Thus K&H transformed into a "help yourself business" where customers waited on themselves. That change gave birth to the check-out stand where instead of listing each item in a charge ledger, the clerk used an adding machine and only entered the total in the ledger, saving both customer and store a lot of time.

The difficulties caused by shortages and rationing affected all Americans, but other aspects of the war touched their lives too. In 1941, with the United States at war for only a few weeks, the end of December was more about Christmas than the war in Benson. The newspaper was full of advertising suggesting gift ideas. Children looked forward to celebrating around the community Christmas tree, where, by tradition, each child received a bag filled with candy, nuts, and fruit.

But by Christmas 1942, the war overshadowed everything. Stores, like the K&H Store, limited purchases of articles that would be difficult to replace to "discourage hoarding and to allow everyone an equal opportunity to obtain supplies." There was no community Christmas tree, breaking a 20 year tradition because there was no candy because there was no sugar. Instead, school kids make wall posters, crossword puzzles, jokes, lapboards, ash trays, and lamp stands as Red Cross projects for air bases, forts, and hospitals.

Christmas 1943, too, was a disappointment for the children. With sugar still in short supply, there was no community tree or bags of goodies for them. The schools held their annual Christmas programs, but a flu epidemic raged for a couple of weeks before Christmas and many were too ill to attend.

After two years of disappointment, the town decided to do something special for the children for Christmas 1944. Mr. and Mrs. Don Hargrave came up the idea of having Santa come to town on his sleigh. Bert Cline, as carpenter, created a sleigh float on a four-wheel trailer, and Santa arrived in style. "When Santa Claus came to town last Friday and Saturday, the children were waiting for him, excited and big-eyed, for it was the first time most of them had seen such a sight; in fact it is doubtful if any of them had seen a sleigh before. One little boy tried to give him a quarter so that he wouldn't forget him and even insisted on having his name written down. Another handed him two nickels and ran away before Santa had a chance to talk him out of it."[224]

The sleigh was carefully dismantled and packed away for use the next year but that didn't happen. In 1945, another flu epidemic cancelled even the school Christmas programs. Besides the flu, outbreaks of colds, chicken pox, scarlet fever, smallpox, measles, mumps, and pink eye plagued both children and adults during the war years. The Christmas programs resumed in 1946, but the community celebration around the tree with gifts for all children was never revived. War had claimed another casualty in the death of this tradition.

A yearly medical problem which has not been previously mentioned is treatment for snake bites, particularly rattlesnake bites. Approximately 150 to 250 people are bitten each year in Arizona by rattlesnakes. Despite the myths about self- treating a bite, being bitten by any venomous snake requires medical attention.

Since Dick (Richard) Hamilton moved to Benson with his family in 1941, he played in the desert as a child, traveled through the desert as an adult, and lived next door to the desert always. In all those years, he hadn't ever seen a rattlesnake. His luck ran out on July 31, 2009 at 8:30 p.m. when he and wife

Bertha were visiting their friends Jim and Kathleen Crawford. As they prepared to leave, Dick stepped out onto the Crawford's porch and felt a double stinging jab to his left ankle.

Dick knew immediately what had happened and hollered for his wife Bertha to rush him to the hospital. He knew that with a snake bite, time is essential, as the deadly venom can travel quickly through the body.

The Western diamondback is responsible for most of the venomous snakebites in North America.

Courtesy U.S. Fish & Wildlife Service.

When he worked at Hamilton Drug in the 1950s, Dick kept a couple of doses of anti-venom in the pharmacy. He remembers a night when Dr. Kartchner called him at home. A young man from a ranch in St. David had been bitten on the hand. His arm had swollen to well over twice its normal size. And as the flesh turns black from the venom, one could watch its progress as it worked its way up the arm. The doctor had already used up his supply of anti-venom on the boy and needed Dick to rush over what doses he had. Their combined doses slowed the venom, but it was still spreading. Dick hopped in his car and frantically drove to Tucson for more. Another two shots stopped the venom just below the shoulder. Had it worked its way past the shoulder, the venom would have gone to the boy's heart.

So Dick was a bit frustrated when his wife was driving

carefully in low gear down the steep hill on Ocotillo and kept yelling at her to drive faster.

When they made it to emergency, the doctor told Dick he had received a "dry bite" and would not need the anti-venom since with a dry bite, the snake releases only a small amount, if any, of poison. Small though it may have been, the flesh on Dick's leg had turned black up to his mid-thigh within ten minutes. A dry bite, the doctor explained, is more of a protective measure by the snake as a warning to get out of the way. And a good thing it was, the doctor added, because had it been a full-blown bite, they would have had to air-lift him to Tucson. While over 50 years earlier both the doctor and the pharmacist stocked anti-venom, in 2009 the hospital did not. That policy changed in 2010 after James Richey became the hospital pharmacist; the hospital began to stock anti-venom again.

Meanwhile the snake's "protective" warning didn't work too well for the rattler, as Jim Crawford killed it. After treating Dick, the doctor called the Crawfords and asked Jim to bring the snake to the hospital. Both Dick and Jim assumed the doctor wanted to examine it. As it turns out, the doctor liked rare and exotic foods. He didn't examine the snake; he cooked and ate it.

Benson also lost three of its major landmarks during the war years, although not due to the war. Both the Mansion Hotel and the Virginia Hotel were torn down in 1942. The Grand Central Hotel built in 1887 had burned to the ground during the 1904 fire. From its ashes rose the Mansion. Jose Casteneda bought the Virginia Hotel in 1888, completely refurbished it, and reopened it in 1889. Both hotels were on 4th Street. The Benson Auditorium on 5th Street had been built in 1914. For 30 years, it served the town as a movie house, dance hall, skating rink, and anything else the town needed it for. It met the wrecking ball in 1944.

War efforts overloaded the nation's infrastructure causing restrictions on travel and communications. The telephone company pleaded with customers not to make unnecessary calls and to restrict the amount of time they spent on the line when making calls. They reminded customers that the same lines they used also carried urgent messages between government offices, military posts, munitions plants, aviation industries, naval bases, shipyards, and factories. "War calls must come first and everyone can cooperate. The telephone company urges that long distance and local calls be brief: that non-essential calls be avoided. Unnecessary conversations may delay essential war calls."[225] Why not just build more lines? "The weight of war on the telephone lines grows heavier every day. We can't build new lines and switchboards to carry the load because copper, aluminum, rubber, and other materials needed for telephone equipment are vital war materials as well."[226]

All priority was given to war traffic; traveling for pleasure was considered a peacetime luxury. By July 1942, travelers had to purchase a ticket in advance and make a reservation to ride the train to avoid overcrowding. The railroad issued a special plea not to take a train during the holiday season because most trains were reserved for furloughs, relatives traveling to meet servicemen, military personnel, and businessmen in war work.

Bette Oldfather recalls the crowded troop trains of those years. "I just remember the great numbers of soldiers. There were little vestibules at the end of each car with just a little sort of bench seat and those would have two or three soldiers crowded there dozing; and of course the seats. You really could not get a ticket to ride ordinarily when these trains were so crowded."[227] Passengers jammed into busses too. For Christmas 1943, "The Wo girls had Christmas dinner all cooked for relatives but no relatives arrived for when their cousins went to get on the bus in Tucson the bus was too heavily loaded with men in the service."[228]

The European conflict ended in May 1945 with the surrender of Germany and Italy, and the Asian conflict in August with the surrender of Japan. President Truman broadcast the official announcement of the end of war on August 14th. Benson celebrated the victory with a free dance at the Benson Feed Store on Tuesday night; businesses closed on Wednesday. Other dances followed at different locations. Dances were popular in Benson, not just for the dancing, but because the activity brought citizens together to celebrate.

Thus far in its ride through history, Benson had changed its identity three times. It began as a railroad town because its location intersected the east/west rail route across the southern part of the U.S. and the north/south route down the San Pedro Valley which gave access to the newly discovered mines to the south. As railroad lines multiplied and the mines played out, railroads moved their terminals to other cities. Railroad workers moved on, and the town's population dropped.

But Benson's location also served another industry. Ranches that dotted the San Pedro Valley corridor brought their cattle to Benson to ship them east or west just as the mines had to ship their ores. As the cattle industry grew to encompass most of the valley, Benson changed into a cattle town. The successful annual rodeo reflected its status. The eventual breakup of the large cattle companies fostered the decline of that industry. But as that was happening, the popularity of automobile travel was growing.

With the development of the highway system, Benson's location once more placed it in an advantageous position. The town had just begun to evolve once more, this time into a travel town, when World War II halted its progress. With the ending of the war and the restrictions on tires, gas, and oil lifted, Americans once more hit the road in their cars and trucks. Benson would profit from their travels and a population increase in the decades to come. Another metamorphosis was underway.

Benson in the late 1940s before the "modern era" ushered in a new growth spurt. Courtesy Bob Nilson.

Household Hints

Because of all the war shortages and difficulties replacing home goods, The *San Pedro Valley News* ran two columns, Household Hints and Around the House, with suggestions for housewives on how to preserve what they had. These are a sampling of those suggestions. In a field test given to women in the 2010s, they were asked to rate the suggestions as good, okay, or poor. The "poor" are not included.

GOOD

"Give house plants on occasional feeding of a teaspoon of bone meal dug into the earth in flower pots."

"French fried potatoes will be more crisp if allowed to stand in cold water for half an hour before frying."

"When preparing oranges for a dessert, pour boiling water over them and let them stand five minutes. This will make them much easier to peel."

"When freshly washed windows are dry, wipe them with tissue paper to make them sparkle."

"A tablespoon of vinegar poured into glue that has become hardened in a bottle will soften it."

"Parsley washed with hot water keeps its flavor better and is easier to chop."

"When plates or dishes are burned after baking, they can be easily cleaned by rubbing them with a cloth dipped in salt."

"Dip fish in milk instead of eggs before rolling in bread or crumbs. The fish will taste better."

"If every housewife in the nation saves as little as 2 tin cans each week, it would mean enough scrap steel to make the steel used in the hulls of 3 heavy cruisers, and the tin used in 20 submarines."

"Alternate the curtains which are exposed to sunlight as the wear will be evenly divided and they will grow old more gracefully."

"Adhesive tape on toe and heel of baby's shoes will keep him from taking a header on the newly waxed floor."

"Wax ashtrays with floor wax to prevent ashes from sticking to tray."

"To flatten rug corners that curl and slip on the floor, cut out L-shaped pieces of cardboard and glue to the underside of the rug at the corners."

"Tie a button on the end of the string attached to the toddler's toy wagon or truck so the string doesn't slip through his fingers."

"If you want to make your letters absolutely sure-seal, glue them shut with colorless nail polish. These can't even be steamed open by unscrupulous persons."

OKAY

"Hard cooked eggs will peel easily if, as soon as they are cooked, their shells are cracked slightly and the eggs are dropped into cold water for five minutes. The eggs may then be chilled and used."

"Don't cut the lemon in half when you want only a few drops of juice. Instead pierce the lemon with a bone knitting needle and squeeze out the amount required. The hole will seal itself."

"Save all celery tops, wash and dry them and place in the oven, turning them now and then. Store the leaves in an airtight tin. Use them for flavoring soups, salads, etc."

"Moist table salt will remove egg tarnish from silver."

"Odors on hands resulting from peeling and slicing onions can be removed by washing the hands in vinegar."

"Mice dislike peppermint. A little oil of peppermint placed around their haunts will soon drive the pests away."

"Honey should be kept in a warm place in the kitchen. If it does granulate, place the container in a pan of hot water until it liquidizes."

"Clean children's teddy bears and like toys by rubbing them with corn starch."

"Add salt to the water in which eggs are to be cooked. This makes the shells more brittle and easier to remove."

"Keep your household sponges fresh by soaking them in cold salt water."

"Before opening a can of paint, turn it upside down for a short time and it will mix better when opened."

"To remove grass stains from white clothes make a paste of baking soda and soap and spread thickly over stain."

"One teaspoon of dissolved gelatin added to one-half pint of whipped cream will make the cream stiffer when whipped."

"A drop of perfume on an electric light bulb will scent the whole room."

"To remove paper that has stuck to a polished surface, soften with a little olive oil."

"Lemon juice, salt, and strong sunlight are cures for stains on white materials."

"When two glasses become wedged together, place cold water in the upper one and set the lower one in warm water. They will then separate with little effort."

"After grating cheese, rub a potato over the grater to clean it."

Mary Lee Tiernan

ENDNOTES

Chapter 1
[1] "Hail to the Chief," *Weekly Arizona Citizen*, October 30, 1880.
[2] "Auction Sale of Lots!" *Weekly Arizona Citizen*, June 19, 1880.
[3] (no title) *Weekly Arizona Citizen*, July 10, 1880.
[4] Palmer, Christena, p. 2.
[5] Sanders, Donnetta C. "White House in Benson Has Bright Purple Past," p. 1.
[6] Colvin, Clara C., p. 1.
[7] Blacklidge, Harry. Letter to Clara Getzwiller, January 11, 1962, p. 1.
[8] Beccetti, Fred. Oral history.

Chapter 2
[9] "From Tucson to Grant," *Arizona Citizen*, Sept. 20, 1983.
[10] Sherlock, p. 2.
[11] Ohnesorgen, *Reminiscences of Wm Ohnesorgen*, p. 3.
[12] Eder, p. 3.
[13] "Benson, Henry McKinley," p. 3.
[14] Eder, p. 1.

Chapter 3
[15] Tellman, p. 7.
[16] "About Fort Huachuca – History."
[17] Underhill, p. 38.
[18] Stevenson, Petra: Oral history, p. 3.
[19] Dobyns, p. 62.
[20] Blacklidge, Letter to Clara Getzwiller, January 11, 1962, p. 1.
[21] Myrick, p. 79.
[22] Underhill, p. 45.
[23] www.tombstoneweb.com
[24] Tellman, p. 26.

[25] Bureau of Land Management. *Fairbank: Historic Townsite.*
[26] Tellman, p. 27.
[27] "About Bisbee."

Chapter 4
[28] (no title) *Arizona Weekly Citizen*, Aug. 21, 1881.
[29] (no title) *Arizona Weekly Citizen*, Sept. 4, 1881.
[30] (no title) *Arizona Weekly Citizen*, Sept. 11, 1881.
[31] Sherlock, p. 3.
[32] "Mansion Hotel Razed," *San Pedro Valley News*, July 9, 1943.
[33] "Benson, June 4, 1882." *Tombstone Epitaph*. June 10, 1882.
[34] "Filing More Suits," *Bisbee Daily Review*, March 30, 1906.
[35] Colvin, no page number.
[36] McGoffin, Geraldine. Oral history.
[37] Myrick p. 107.
[38] "Tombstone Nugget." *Arizona Sentinel*, Aug. 27, 1881.
[39] "The Benson Rustlers." *Tombstone Epitaph.*
[40] Ibid.
[41] https://tombstoneweb.com/history/
[42] "Man Is Killed in Saloon Row," *Bisbee Daily Review*, Dec. 1, 1906.
[43] Ibid.
[44] "A Fatal Shooting," *Graham Guardian*, May 9, 1902.
[45] "Shepard Keeps Still," *Bisbee Daily Review*, May 9, 1902.
[46] "Jury's Verdict," *Bisbee Daily Review*, May 7, 1902.
[47] O'Neal, Bill, *Captain Harry Wheeler: Arizona Lawman*, p. 41.
[48] "A Fatal Killing," *Tombstone Epitaph*, March 3, 1907.
[49] "Wheeler Gives Statement to Press," *Bisbee Daily Review*, March 6, 1907.
[50] Ibid.
[51] "Constable Frank Trask Murdered by a Tramp," *Tombstone Epitaph*, May 14, 1911.
[52] Ibid.
[53] Benjamin, p. 4.

Chapter 5
[54] Ohnesorgen, *Reminiscences of an Arizona Pioneer*, p. 10.
[55] "Benson Reduction Works," *Arizona Weekly Citizen*, Aug. 13, 1881.
[56] (no title) *Arizona Weekly Citizen*, Aug. 4, 1883.
[57] "Personal Mention," *Arizona Weekly Citizen*, Oct. 9, 1881.

[58] "The School at Benson," *Tombstone Epitaph*, Nov. 4, 1882.
[59] "The Result of Dr. Gregory's Visit to Benson," *Arizona Weekly Citizen*, Aug. 6, 1882.
[60] (no title) *Arizona Weekly Citizen*, Sept. 22, 1883.
[61] "Benson Herself Again," *Arizona Weekly Citizen*, Oct. 6, 1883, reprinted from the *Benson Herald*.
[62] "Weekly Mining Review," *Arizona Weekly Citizen*, Nov. 17, 1883.
[63] "Benson Items," *Daily Tombstone Epitaph*, Jan. 21, 1885.
[64] (no title) *Mohave Country Miner*, June 8, 1889.
[65] (no title) *Tombstone Daily Prospector*, Feb 4, 1889.
[66] Jennings, p. 1.
[67] "Benson Burnt," *Daily Tombstone*, May 10, 1886.
[68] "Benson," *Arizona Weekly Citizen*, July 24, 1886.
[69] Rogers, Eugene, p. 17.
[70] Tellman, p. 47.
[71] Ibid.
[72] "The Grand Central Hotel," *Arizona Daily Orb*, April 28, 1900.
[73] "A Grand Reception," *Tombstone Epitaph*, April 26, 1891.

Chapter 6
[74] "Benson Public Library," *The Cochise County Historical Journal:* Spring/Summer 2000, p. 26.
[75] Ibid., p. 27.
[76] "The Result of Dr. Gregory's Visit to Benson," *Arizona Weekly Citizen*, Aug. 6, 1882.
[77] "Weekly Champion," *The Arizona Champion*, Feb. 2, 1884.
[78] (no title) *Tombstone Epitaph*, June 7, 1893.
[79] (no title) *Tombstone Epitaph*, Nov. 18, 1894.
[80] Cox, Sharilyn Rogers. "Hi Wo Grocery Opened in 1896." *The Cochise County Historical Journal:* Spring/Summer 2000, p. 22.
[81] "Leonard D. Redfield." *The Cochise County Historical Journal:* Spring/Summer 2000, p. 52.
[82] Blacklidge, Harry. Letter to Clara Getzwiller.
[83] Dobyns, p. 79.
[84] Petra Stevenson, Oral history.

Chapter 7
[85] Powell, Janice L. "Dr. C.C Powell and The Powell House." *The Cochise County Historical Journal*: Spring/Summer 1998, p. 18.

[86] Sanders, Donnette C., "White House in Benson Has Purple Past."
[87] "A Fatal Shooting," *Graham Guardian*, May 9, 1902.
[88] "Shepard Keeps Still." *Bisbee Daily Review*, May 9, 1902.
[89] "Jury's Verdict." *Bisbee Daily Review*, May 7, 1902.
[90] "Copper Production of AZ Mines, the *Daily Arizona Silver Belt*, July 24, 1908.
[91] "News Briefs," *The Oasis,* 1903.
[92] "Improvements at Benson." *Bisbee Daily Review*, July 10, 1902.
[93] "Industrial School Opening," *Graham Guardian*, Dec. 11, 1903.
[94] "Brick Making Begins at Benson." *Bisbee Daily Review*, Dec. 15, 1901.
[95] (no title) *Tombstone Epitaph*, Sept. 15, 1901.
[96] Rogers, W. Lane, "Hotel Arnold."
[97] "The Water Discovery Shows the Possibilities of This Important Feature." *Cochise Review*, August 20, 1900.
[98] "Benson Water Co." *Bisbee Daily Review*, Oct. 5, 1905.
[99] "Benson, AZ Train Wreck Dec 1909."
http:www3.gendisasters.com/Arizona/4830/
[100] Sherlock, p. 3.

Chapter 8

[101] Sherlock, p. 3.
[102] Larson, Louise. A History ... p. 105.
[103] *Superintendent's Annual Report of the Territorial Industrial School: June 30, 1911.*
[104] "Princely Gift to Benson School Dist.," *Tombstone Epitaph*, April 5, 1914.
[105] Tellman, p. 20.
[106] Ibid.
[107] Ibid.
[108] Geraldine McGoffin, Oral history.
[109] (no title) *Tombstone Epitaph*, Sept. 2, 1894.
[110] Shortridge, Harold, "The Benson and Cochise County Adventure," Oral history.
[111] Editorial, *Benson Signal*, Sept. 23, 1916.
[112] "Will Put On Moving Picture Show," *The Benson Signal*, Feb. 12, 1916.
[113] Editorial, *Benson Signal*, Sept. 2, 1916.

Benson's Ride through History: 1880 - 1945

[114] Shortridge, Harold. "The Benson and Cochise County Adventure," Oral history.
[115] "Local Items," *Benson Signal*, July 18, 1917.
[116] "Local Items," *Benson Signal*, Aug. 7, 1915.
[117] "Local Items," *Benson Signal*, Dec. 4, 1915.
[118] "Local Items," *Benson Signal*, Sept. 18, 1915.
[119] "Local Items," *Benson Signal*, Sept. 18, 1915.
[120] "Local Items," *Benson Signal*, May 12, 1916.
[121] "Local Items," *Benson Signal*, October 6, 1916.
[122] "Local Items," *Benson Signal*, Dec. 4, 1915.
[123] "Local Items," *Benson Signal*, Oct. 28, 1916.
[124] "Local Items," *Benson Signal*, March 18, 1916.
[125] "Local Items," *Benson Signal*, Sept. 18, 1915.
[126] "False Alarm," *Benson Signal*, April 21, 1916.
[127] "Local Items," *Benson Signal*, June 3, 1916.
[128] "Monument to the Memory of Old Dr. J.N. Morrison, A." The San Pedro Valley Arts & Historical Society: Vertical File.
[129] Clea Curtis Brown, Oral history.
[130] "Local Items," *Benson Signal*, June 9, 1917.
[131] Editorial, *Benson Signal*, June 16, 1917.
[132] Editorial, *Benson Signal*, June 16, 1917.
[133] "Local Items: Notice," *Benson Signal*, June 2, 1917.
[134] "Local Items: Notice." *Benson Signal*, June 17, 1916.
[135] "Local Items," *Benson Signal*, May 26, 1917.
[136] "Local Items," *Benson Signal*, Aug. 18, 1917.
[137] Arizona Dept. of Liquor.
[138] "Constable John Proffitt Makes Haul," *Benson Signal*, Nov. 6, 1915.
[139] "Prohibition Helps the Workingman Says Mining Delegate," *Benson Signal*, Sept. 9, 1916.
[140] "News Briefs," *Benson Signal*, Jan. 1, 1917.
[141] "Lost or Stolen," *Benson Signal*, Dec. 4, 1915.
[142] "Lost or Stolen," *Benson Signal*, Dec. 22, 1917.
[143] "Local Items." *Benson Signal*, Jan. 27, 1917.

Chapter 9
[144] "Accident Results in Revelation." *Benson News*, March 2, 1928.
[145] Editorial. *Benson News*, Feb 10, 1928.
[146] "Tricks of the Trade." *Benson News*, March 9, 1928.

[147] Amy Lowery, Oral history.
[148] Mabel Barrow, Oral history.
[149] Chauncey T. Jones, Oral history.
[150] "It Is a Pleasing Picture for Mrs. Rosa M. Schwab." *San Pedro Valley News*, Sept. 18, 1942.
[151] "Local Items." *Benson News*, Sept. 9, 1927.
[152] "Local Items." *Benson News*, June 1, 1928.
[153] "Local Items." *Benson News*, August 3, 1928.
[154] "Local Items." *Benson News*, July 17, 1928.
[155] "Hobos Out of Luck." *Benson News*, March 30, 1928. p. 1.
[156] Tellman, p. 47.
[157] Dobyns, p. 159.
[158] Katherine Mejia, Oral history.

Chapter 10
[159] Carl Haupt, Oral history.
[160] Larson, *A History...* pp. 428-429.
[161] Carl Haupt, Oral history.
[162] Katherine Darnell, Oral history.
[163] "Throw Away Day," *San Pedro Valley News*, April 17, 1931.
[164] Editorial. *San Pedro Valley News*, Feb. 6, 1931.
[165] Carl Haupt, Oral history.
[166] Vay Fenn, Oral history.
[167] "The Meanest Thief Found in Benson," *San Pedro Valley News*, Jan. 5, 1934.
[168] *The Cochise County Historical Journal, Spring/Summer 2000*, p. 53.
[169] "Thief Gets Voting Booth," *San Pedro Valley News*, Sept. 21, 1934.
[170] "For Rent." *San Pedro Valley News,* March, 1934.
[171] "For Rent." *San Pedro Valley News,* Nov. 1935.
[172] "For Rent." *San Pedro Valley News,* April 3, 1936.
[173] "For Rent." *San Pedro Valley News,* April 24, 1936.
[174] "For Rent." *San Pedro Valley News,* Dec. 3, 1937.
[175] "News Briefs." *San Pedro Valley News*, Oct. 28, 1938.
[176] "Building Fences to Keep Out Cattle," *San Pedro Valley News*, Oct. 20, 1939.
[177] Tellman, p. 30.
[178] Sherlock, p. 4.
[179] "Apache Powder Co. Has Never Cut Pay," *San Pedro Valley News*, Sept. 1, 1933, p.1.

Benson's Ride through History: 1880 - 1945

[180] Ray Kenworthy, Oral history.
[181] Vay Fenn, Oral history.
[182] "Youth Killed by Fall from Freight Train," *San Pedro Valley News*, June 12, 1931.
[182] "Quarantine Is Declared for Measles and Mumps," *San Pedro Valley News*, Feb. 21, 1936.
[183] "News Briefs." *San Pedro Valley News*, Sept. 29, 1931.
[184] "News Briefs." *San Pedro Valley News*, Feb. 5, 1937.
[185] "Paralysis Causes Schools to Close," *San Pedro Valley News*, Oct. 5, 1934.
[186] "News Briefs." *San Pedro Valley News*, Oct. 19, 1934.
[187] Editorial comment. *San Pedro Valley News,* March 6, 1931.
[188] Editorial comment. *San Pedro Valley News,* Aug. 20, 1937.
[189] "Personal." *San Pedro Valley News,* Jan. 6, 1933.
[190] "The Neighborhood." *San Pedro Valley News,* Nov. 1, 1935.
[191] "Gila Monster Is Victorious in Battle with Rattlesnake," *San Pedro Valley News*, Oct. 16, 1931.
[192] "Personal." San Pedro Valley News, July 7, 1939.
[193] "About the Dust Bowl," p. 3.
[194] Editorial. *San Pedro Valley News*, April 7, 1939.
[195] Depression in the United States... p.5.

Chapter 11

[196] Note that "show" was not part of the title.
[197] https://wikipedia.org/wiki/Buffalo_Bill#Buffalo_Bill's_Wild_West
[198] Virgil Haverty, Oral history.
[199] (title missing) *San Pedro Valley News*, Sept. 8, 1939.
[200] "Jockey Dies As Result of Accident at Benson Rodeo," *San Pedro Valley News*, September 5, 1947.
[201] "Lease Oasis Camp to Army Wives," *San Pedro Valley News*, August 21, 1942.
[202] "Benson Rodeo Continues High Pre-War Standard," *San Pedro Valley News*, September 8, 1944.

Chapter 12

[203] "A Little Safety Talk," *San Pedro Valley News*, Aug 23, 1940.
[204] Sunday school announcement, *San Pedro Valley News*, August 23, 1940.

[205] "Seen and Heard Around Town," *San Pedro Valley News*, January 12, 1940.
[206] Dobyns, p. 170.
[207] https://www.gamblingsites.com
[208] "Earthquake Felt Here in Benson Saturday Night," *San Pedro Valley News*, May 24, 1940.
[209] "This Week in Defense," *San Pedro Valley News*, November 29, 1940.
[210] "This Week in Defense." *San Pedro Valley News*, August 8, 1941.
[211] "Apache Powder Gives Bonus Checks." *San Pedro Valley News*, March 14, 1941.
[212] "Help Wanted," *San Pedro Valley News*, October 3, 1941.
[213] Letter from Louis Robinson, *San Pedro Valley News*, July 19, 1940.
[214] "U.S. Declares War on Germany, Italy; Sink Jap Ship at Wake," *San Pedro Valley News*, December 12, 1941, p. 1.
[215] "Seen and Heard Around Town," *San Pedro Valley News*, May 8, 1942.
[216] "Seen and Heard Around Town," *San Pedro Valley News*, August 20, 1943.
[217] Advertisement, *San Pedro Valley News*, May 19, 1944.
[218] "Seen and Heard Around Town," *San Pedro Valley News*, June 15, 1945.
[219] www.u-s-history.com/pages/h1674.htm *US Treasury Bonds*
[220] Letter to Senator Carl Hayden. *San Pedro Valley News*, June 1, 1945.
[221] www.u-s-history.com/pages/h1674.htm *US Treasury Bonds*
[222] Letter from Louis Robinson, *San Pedro Valley News*, Published Jan 2, 1942; dated Dec. 22, 1941.
[223] www.u-s-history.com/pages/h1682.htm *U.S. War Bonds*
[224] "Benson Children Nearly Mob Santa Claus," *San Pedro Valley News*, Dec. 29, 1944.
[225] "This Week in Defense," *San Pedro Valley News*, Sept. 11, 1942.
[226] "This Week in Defense," *San Pedro Valley News*, Aug. 8, 1942.
[227] Bette Oldfather, Oral history.
[228] "Seen and Heard Around Town," *San Pedro Valley News*, Jan. 1, 1943.

BIBLIOGRAPHY

Section 1
Newspaper sources are listed in Section 2.

"1903 News Briefs from the Benson Press." *San Pedro Valley News-Sun: Second Annual Historical Edition.* March 1972. p. 14.

1921 Remember When...A Nostalgic Look Back in Time. Birmingham, Alabama: Seek Publishing.

1922 Remember When...A Nostalgic Look Back in Time. Birmingham, Alabama: Seek Publishing.

1934 Remember When...A Nostalgic Look Back in Time. Birmingham, Alabama: Seek Publishing.

1944 Remember When...A Nostalgic Look Back in Time. Birmingham, Alabama: Seek Publishing.

"About Bisbee." www.bisbeearizona.com

"About Fort Huachuca - History." www.huachuca.army.mil

"About the Dust Bowl."
http://www.english.illinois.edu/maps/depression/dustbowl.htm.

"Adventists Rebuilt Presbyterian Church." *News-Sun Centennial Edition*, March 20, 1980, p. 39.

Apache Nitrogen Products, Inc. St. David, Arizona.

"Apache Powder Company and the Railroads." January 25, 1981. The San Pedro Valley Arts & Historical Society: Apache Powder Company file.

"Apache Powder Company Is Essential." The San Pedro Valley Arts & Historical Society: Apache Powder Company file.

Arizona Business Directory: 1905-1908. Benson section, pp. 110-115.

"Arizona State Route 80."
https://en.wikipedia.org/wiki/Arizona_State_Route_80

Bailey, Lynn R. and Don Chaput. *Cochise County Stalwarts. Vol. One: A-K.* Tucson, Arizona: Westernlore Press, 2000.

---. *Cochise County Stalwarts. Vol. Two: L-Z*. Tucson, Arizona: Westernlore Press, 2000.

Barnes, Will C. *Arizona Name Places*. Tucson, AZ: University of Arizona. January 1, 1935. p. 44.

---. *Arizona Name Places*. 1960. Revised and enlarged by Byrd H. Granger. 1977. Tucson, AZ: University of Arizona. p. 30.

Beitler, Stu, contributor. "Benson, AZ Train Wreck, Dec.1909." www3.gendisasters.com/arizona...

Benjamin, Stan. *Benson, Arizona: One Hundred Years of Law Enforcement*. Tucson, Arizona: Feb. 2000.

"Benson, AZ Train Wreck, Dec 1909." http:www3.gendisasters.com/Arizona/4830/

Benson General and Business Directory: 1883-1884. Cobler & Co.

"Benson, Henry McKinley." www.asu.edu/lib/archives/azbio/bios/BENSON-H. p. 3.

"Benson Powder Depot Blast Leaves 4 Dead." January 12, 1948. The San Pedro Valley Arts & Historical Society: Apache Powder Company file.

"Benson, William H." *Portrait and Biographical Records of Arizona*. Chicago, Illinois: Chapman Publishing Co. 1901.

Benton-Cohen, Katherine. *Borderline Americans: Racial Division and Labor War in the Arizona Borderlands*. Cambridge, Massachusetts: Harvard University Press. 2009.

"Big Nose Kate, The Shady Ladies, and The 1880's Bordellos." http://www.bignosekates.info\History\Big Nose Kate, The Shady Ladies, and The 1880's Bordellos

"Bisbee History." www.discoverbisbee.com

Black Blizzard: The Storm at the Heart of the Great Depression. History Channel. Television show aired February 3, 2012.

Blacklidge, Harry J. Letter to Clara Getzwiller dated January 11, 1962. The San Pedro Valley Arts & Historical Society. Vertical File: Trask Family.

---. Undated, handwritten document. The San Pedro Valley Arts & Historical Society. Benson Tidbits.

Brenner, Elizabeth. "The Legend is a Historical Fact..." *Benson Butterfield Rodeo*. Pamphlet. October 11, 2008.

"Brenner Furniture." Advertisement. *The San Pedro Valley News-Sun Centennial Edition*, March 20, 1980, p. 5.

"Buffalo Bill's Wild West."
https://wikipedia.org/wiki/Buffalo_Bill#Buffalo_Bill's_Wild_West

Bureau of Land Management. *Fairbank: Historic Townsite.* Pamphlet.

Business Directories: loose pages without bibliographic notations for Benson from 1880-1881, 1881, 1883, and 1930.

Business Telephone Directory - Year 1928: Arizona; El Paso County, Texas; New Mexico. El Paso, Texas: The Mountain States Telephone and Telegraph Company. 1928.

Cavanaugh, Wade. "Engineers Didn't Know Conductor Had Jumped." *San Pedro Valley News-Sun.* June 1973.

Chamberlain, D.S. "Tombstone in 1879: The Lighter Side." *The Journal of Arizona History.* Tucson: Arizona Historical Society. Winter, 1972. pp. 229-234.

Civilian Conservation Corps (CCC).
http://en.wikipedia/.org/wiki/Civilian_Conservation_Corps.

Cochise County Historical Journal. Vol. 28, No.1. Spring/Summer 1998.

---. Vol. 30, No.1. Spring/Summer 2000, p. 53.

Cole, Dana. "Butterfield adds new activities." *San Pedro Valley News-Sun.* October 5, 2011. pp. A1 & A7.

---. "Old-time UPRR steam engine to stop in Benson." *San Pedro Valley News-Sun.* November 2, 2011. pp. A1 & A8.

Colvin, Clara C. Untitled, undated, typewritten document. The San Pedro Valley Arts & Historical Society. Benson Tidbits.

Davis, Elmer E. "The Only Arizona Industry of Its Kind - Some Interesting Facts." *The Mining Congress Journal.* November 1925. Reprinted copy in The San Pedro Valley Arts & Historical Society: Apache Powder Company file.

"Depression in the United States: An Overview, The. (Great Depression)
http://www.english.illinois.edu/maps/depression/overview.htm.

"Destruction Fire: Five Business Houses Are Now Ruins." Nov. 14, 1904. The San Pedro Valley Arts & Historical Society: Vertical File, Fires.

Dobyns, Henry F. and Theodore Bundy, James E. Officer, and Richard W. Stoffle. *Los Tres Alamos Del Rio San Pedro: The Peculiar Persistence of a Place Name.* Tucson, Arizona: Pinon Press. 1996. Manuscript form.

Duncan, Chuck: Kartchner Caverns Park Ranger. Personal interview by Mary Lee Tiernan. November 28, 2011.

"Earthquake of 1877." Palominas Area History. www.palominas.com

Eatherly, Charles R. "History of Kartchner Caverns State Park." http://azstateparks.com/parkskaca/history

Eder, Clara Ann. "Telling It Like It Was ... A History of Benson." *San Pedro Valley News-Sun: Second Annual Historical Edition*. March 1972. pp. 3-5.

---. "Huachuca Street carries long, varied history." *New-Sun Centennial Edition*, March 29, 1980, p.19.

---. "The Little Old Graveyard at Benson." Manuscript.

Egerton, Kearney. "The Grand Finale of Benson's Jack-the-Ripper." August 19, 1979. The San Pedro Valley Arts & Historical Society: Vertical File, Jack the Ripper.

Ellsworth, Edward. *Benson Pioneer Cemetery: Benson, Azizona.*

Ellsworth, Edward. Personal interview by Mary Lee Tiernan. September 22, 2011.

Fenn, Alvah (Vay). Personal interview by Mary Lee Tiernan. Dec. 8, 2010.

Frega, A.M. *The Hub City: Benson, Arizona.* Benson, Arizona. July 2018.

Friends of Kartchner Caverns State Park. *The Jewel of the Desert*. Tucson, Arizona. 1999. DVD, 47 minutes.

Fry, Norm. *Those Damn Apaches*. The San Pedro Valley Arts & Historical Society: Apache Powder Company file.

Gambling sites. https://www.gamblingsites.com

Glenn, Erik and Cori Dolan. "Arizona's Open Range 'Law'." *Excerpt from the University of Arizona Cooperative Extension Publication AZ1533,* Dec. 2010. https://extension.arizona.edu/sites/extension.arizona.edu/files/pubs/az1533.pdf

Granger, Bryd Howell. *Arizona's Names: X Marks the Spot*. Tucson, Arizona: The Falconer Publishing Co. 1983. pp. 59-60.

Hamilton, Richard (Dick). Personal interview by Mary Lee Tiernan. Dec. 6, 2010.

Hendricks, Janice. "The Day the Earth Shook." *Tombstone Times*. May 2005. pp.1, 4, 5.

"History of Tombstone, A." www.tombstoneweb.com

"How Times Change." The San Pedro Valley Arts & Historical Society: Vertical File, Doctors.

"Improvement Committee Precedes Chamber." *The San Pedro Valley News-Sun* Centennial Edition, March 20, 1980, p. 3.

"James and Lois Kartchner and the Kartchner Caverns." *Cochise County Historical Journal.* Spring/Summer 1998. pp. 38-43.

Jennings, Marguerite. "$150,000 Benson Fire Stirs Memories of Earlier Blazes." The San Pedro Valley Arts & Historical Society: Vertical File, Fires.

Johnson, Raymond (Ray). Personal interview by Mary Lee Tiernan. Dec. 7, 2010.

Jones, Max. Personal interview by Mary Lee Tiernan. January 4, 2011.

Jones, Max D. Retired Fire Chief. *The History of Benson Volunteer Fire Department 1907-2007.* March 2007.

Kartchner, Dean and Max. Personal interview by Mary Lee Tiernan. October 6, 2011.

Kartchner, Gary. Personal interview by Mary Lee Tiernan. January 13, 2011.

"Kennedy Was an Arizona Laborer! – 27 Years Ago." *The Phoenix Gazette.* July 26, 1963.

Kleine, Jack. Personal interview by Mary Lee Tiernan. Dec. 15, 2010.

KUAT Communications Group. *The Desert Speaks: Sensitive Species.* Video, 28 minutes. Tucson, Arizona: University of Arizona. 1995.

Land, Rose Veselak. "A Brief Essay on Medicine in Territorial Arizona 1846-1909 especially in Benson/San Pedro Valley environs." The San Pedro Valley Arts & Historical Society: Vertical File, Doctors.

Land records for Peter Church and Jacob Horsch. www.glorecords.blm.gov.

Larson, Louise Fenn. *A House by the Side of the Road: Memoirs Alvah and Carmen Forster Fenn.* Mesa, Arizona: Cox Printing. 2005.

---. *Pomerene, Arizona and the Valley of the San Pedro: A History.* Mesa, Arizona: Cox Printing. 1999.

Lee, Ed. Personal interview by Mary Lee Tiernan. January 4, 2011.

Lodzinski, John. "How did Benson get its name?" *San Pedro Valley News-Sun.* September 28, 2011. pp. A4-5.

Loring, William H. "The 1887 Earthquake." *Cochise County Quarterly*, Vol 18, No. 1. Spring 1988. pp.41-44.

Los Triaditos. Display panels at museum. The San Pedro Valley Arts & Historical Society.

Lutrell, Estelle. *Newspapers and Periodicals of Arizona 1859-1911.* Tucson, Arizona: University of Arizona Press. 1950. pp. 15-16.

Mayberry, Carter M.D. Personal interview by Mary Lee Tiernan. January 25, 2012.

Mccool, Grance. "Rails brought residents to Benson." *News-Sun Centennial Edition*, March 20, 1980, p. 24.

McGarvin, Thomas G. "The 1887 Sonoran Earthquake: It Wasn't Our Fault." AZ Bureau of Geology & Mineral Technology FIELDNOTES, Summer 1987, p. 1.

Merrill, Frank. Personal interview by Mary Lee Tiernan. January 7, 2011.

Miller, Neil. *Kartchner Caverns: How Two Cavers Discovered and Saved One of the Wonders of the Natural World.* Tucson, Arizona: The University of Arizona Press. 2008.

Myrick, David F. *Railroads of Arizona, Vol. I: the Southern Roads.* Berkeley, CA: Howell-North Books. 1975.

National Youth Administration (NYA). http://en.wikipedia/.org/wiki/National_Youth_Administration.

Negri, Sam. *Nature's Underground Wonderland: Kartchner Caverns State Park.* Department of Transportation, Arizona. 1998, fourth printing 2005.

Nilson, Bob. "History of Benson." Benson, AZ: Cochise College, Lecture. March 28, 2011.

San Pedro Valley News-Sun: 100 Years in a Railroad Town. Special Centennial Edition. March 20, 1980. 48 pp.
  "Adventists rebuilt Presbyterian church." p. 39.
  "Presbyterian Church formed by members in 1904." p. 39.

"Monument to the Memory of Old Dr. J.N. Morrison, A." The San Pedro Valley Arts & Historical Society: Vertical File.

Old Benson Library Served Many Uses at 'Total Wreck' Mine Camp." The San Pedro Valley Arts & Historical Society: Vertical File.

Ohnesorgen, William. Personal interview by Mrs. George Kitt. January 12 (no year given). *Reminiscences of an Arizona Pioneer: Personal Experiences of William Ohnesorgen.*

--- *Reminiscences of William Ohnesorgen* as told to Mrs. George F. Kitt. October 22, 1929.

Oldfather, Bette. "The San Pedro Valley Scene." *The San Pedro Valley News-Sun.* Sept. 29, 1977. p. 8.

O'Neal, Bill. The Arizona Rangers. Austin, Texas: Eakin Press. 1987. pp. 111-115.

---. *Captain Harry Wheeler: Arizona Lawman.* Austin, Texas: Eakin Press. 2003. pp. 41-44.

O'Neil, Harry E. "Tres Alamos: A Place Forgotten." *The Cochise County Historical Journal.* Vol. 35, No.2. Fall/Winter 2005.

"Ordinance Number Thirty Six." City of Benson Records. Dec. 2, 1935.

Orozco, Rebecca. "The Life of a Woman Homesteader." Benson, AZ: Cochise College, Lecture. March 21, 2011.

"Pacific Railroad Survey." www.pointtopointsurvey.com

"Pacific Railroad Survey." www.ezinearticles.com

Palmer, Christena. "The Real Life of Prostitutes in the Old West." www.associatedcontent.com

Parker, Lowell. "Gunfight Site Now a Prosaic Tax Office." The San Pedro Valley Arts & Historical Society: Vertical File, Jack the Ripper.

Parker, Lowell. "Stingy Bonus Got Jack the Ripper Shot." The San Pedro Valley Arts & Historical Society: Vertical File, Jack the Ripper.

Poliomyelitis. http://en.wikipedia.org/wiki/History_of_poliomyelitis.

Porier, Shar. "Quake myths busted: Carr House speaker shares facts about major 1887 event." *Sierra Vista Herald/The Bisbee Daily Review.* July 25, 2007.

Powell, Janice L. "Dr. C.C Powell and the Powell House." *The Cochise County Historical Journal,* Spring/Summer 1998, p. 18.

"Presbyterian Church Formed by Members in 1904." *News-Sun Centennial Edition,* March 20, 1980, p. 39.

"Public Library Followed Reading Room." Excerpt from the Benson Press 1903. *San Pedro Valley News-Sun: Second Annual Historical Edition.* March 1972. p. 23.

Ralph Comey Architects and Janet H. Strittmatter, Inc. *Historic Resources Inventory & Report of the Benson Historic Barrio.* Tucson, Arizona. September 30, 2005.

"Reading Room Assured." Excerpt from the Benson Press 1903. *San Pedro Valley News-Sun: Second Annual Historical Edition.* March 1972. p. 23.

"Remnants of Benson Highway still standing."
https://arizonasonoranewsservice.com/remnants-of-benson-highway-still-standing/

Rogers, Eugene F. *Merchandising Memoirs.* Manuscript. p. 17.

Rogers, Sharilyn. "Pioneers survive sad arrival in San Pedro Valley." *News-Sun Centennial Edition,* March 20, 1980.

Rogers, W. Lane. "Earthquake." *Arizona Range News*. December 10, 2008.

---. "Hotel Arnold." *San Pedro Valley News-Sun*, May 7, 2008.

Rose, John D. "J.D. Kinnear's Stage Station." www.wyattearpexplorers.com

Rudd, Marie. "Apache Nitrogen celebrates 75 years in Benson this year." *San Pedro Valley News-Sun*. May 24, 1995. p. 6.

"San Pedro flood wiped out bridges and roads." *San Pedro Valley News-Sun Centennial Edition*, March 20, 1980.

San Pedro Valley Arts & Historical Society / Benson History Museum. Benson Tidbits, clippings file.

San Pedro Valley Arts & Historical Society / Benson History Museum. Oral Histories Collection.

VOLUME A-B, Book 1:
  Aguirre, Mary Belle Barnard
  Baker, Sammy
  Barnes, Will C.
  Barrow, Mabel
  Bearse, Loring
  Becchetti, Fred
  Bernal Sr., Hilbert
  Bingham, Audrey
  Black, Baxter
  Brown, Albert
  Brown, Clea
  Browning, Betsy
  Bundy, Winifred
  Burton, Ruth Choate
  Butler, Carolina C. (with Mary Quihuiz Lopez and Ramona Trujillo)
  Lowery, Amy (sic)
  Shortridge, Harold (sic)

VOLUME C-E, Book 2:
  Castaneda, Jose Miguel
  Cemetery, Seventh Street
  Bingham, Audrey
  Comstock, Clifton and Mildred
  Coons, Clifford (Shorty)
  Crawford, Elizabeth

Benson's Ride through History: 1880 - 1945

   Darnell, Katherine
   Dibble, Wanda
   Dreyfuss, Thomas
   Dunbar, Thomas
   Dunbar Smith, Monica
   Eavenson, Wallace
   Ellsworth, Edward
   Ellsworth, William Ephriam

VOLUME F-H, Book 3:
   Fenn, Vay
   Frick, Susan Adair DeRosier
   Gamez, Beatrice F.
   Gamez, Beatriz Castelum
   Gamez, Bernardo S.
   Garrison, Jim
   Getzwiller, Donaletta
   Gordon, Shiela and Gray
   Guerra, William
   Hales, Harvey
   Hamilton, Richard
   Haupt, Carl F.
   Haverty, Virgil
   Hellwig daughters: Julia (Judy) Jones, Martha Nicolson,
      Mary Jane Ridgeway, Betty Wyatt.
   Herrmann, Anne
   Hi Wo
   Hoskinson, Gerald
   Husband, Liz

VOLUME I-L, Book 4:
   Ivey, Jr., J.A.
   Jarvis, Mary Elizabeth
   Jennings, Marguerite
   Jones, Chauncey T.
   Kartchner, Lois
   Keith, Ada
   Kennedy, John F.
   Kenworthy, Ray
   Kleine, Jack
   Land, Rose Veselak

Larson, Louise Fenn
Lee, Matt
Lee, Page
Lopez, Mary Quihuiz and Teresa Mendivi Gradillas
Lowery, Amy.

VOLUME M-N, Book 5:
McGoffin, Geraldine (Gerry)
McMinimy, George
McMinimy, Wanda
Mc Rae, Jack and Flora
Martin, Armida Calderon Romero
Mejia, Katherine
Miller, Gwendolyn
Moncada, Eulalia (Lolly) Quihuiz
Montgomery, John
Monzingo, Peg
Naegle, Carl and Marguerite Jennings
Naegle, Lynn

VOLUME O-P-Q-R, Book 6:
Ohnesorgen, Dora and Donaleta Getzwiller and Audrey Bingham
Ohnesorgen, William
Oldfather, Betty
Oldfather, Miles
Palma, Tony and Audrey
Pennington, Ida Lee Lancaster
Phinney, Chad
Post, Jack
Presidents San Pedro Valley Arts & Historical Society: Alain Hartmann, Elizabeth Brenner, and Gloria Saunders
Quinn, Irene Leneau
Richards, Christina

VOLUME S, Book 7:
Schmazel, Lucille and Ann Herrmann
Searle, Geneva Lewis
Shanefelt, Sunny Beverly
Sherman, Bruce and Geneva
Shilling, Arthur T.
Shortridge, Harold
Sierakowsky, Joe

Smith, A.G. and Mary W.
Smith, Betty Lou Durham
Smith, James
Stephens, Perry Joseph and Catherine (Kitty) E.
Stevenson, Petra Figueroa
Sunderland, Nedra.
VOLUME T, V, W, Z, Book 8:
Talley, Mabel (Ida)
Thomas, Odell
Venable, Genevieve
Wagner, Ida Williams
Wattles, Jeanne
Webb, Paul and Oda May
Whaley, Lorene
Wilharm, Peter and Patricia
Williams, Bill and Effie
Williams, Jane
Wo, Soledad and Isabel and Victoria
Woolsey, Ed
Zupic, Emma Marshall

Sanborn Map and Publishing Company. New York: July 1886. Fire maps.

Sanborn Map Company. New York: March 1909, February 1931. Fire maps.

Sanborn-Perris Map Company. New York: November 1890, May 1898, April 1901. Fire maps.

Sanders, Donnetta C. "Legends Evolve Around Outcast Graves." *The Arizona Republic.* Phoenix, Arizona. March 10, 1968.

---. "White House in Benson Has Bright Purple Past." *The Arizona Republic.* San Pedro Valley Arts & Historical Society, The. Benson Tidbits, clippings file.

Schalau, Jeff, Agent. "Backyard Gardner: Arizona's Open Range Laws." *Agriculture & Natural Resources, University of Arizona Cooperative Extension, Yavapai County*, Oct. 10, 2012.
https://cals.arizona.edu/yavapai/anr/hort/byg/archive/azopenrangelaws.html

Scott, Mary E. "Benson's Old Time Dr. Morrison Does Successful Bone Surgery." The San Pedro Valley Arts & Historical Society: Vertical File, Doctors.

Sherlock, Basil J. "Community Change in the Southwest: The Case of Benson." *Arizona Review of Business and Public Administration: Bureau of Business and Public Research.* Vol. 12, No. 9. September 1963. pp. 1-10.

Shortridge, Harold. "The Benson and Cochise County Adventure." Oral History.

Shull, Kathleen. "Richard Hamilton closes pharmacy." *The San Pedro Valley News-Sun.* July 24, 1996.

Southern Arizona Transportation Museum. 414 N. Toole Avenue, Tucson, Arizona.

"Southern Pacific Railroad." www.trainweb.org/highdeserttrails

"SSVEC Adapts to Changing Needs." *News-Sun Centennial Edition*, March 20, 1980, p. 38.

Stein, Pat H. *Homesteading in Arizona 1870-1942.* Phoenix, AZ: Arizona State Historic Preservation Office. August, 1990.

Suagee, E. Kathy and the San Pedro Valley Arts and Historical Society. *Images of America: Around Benson.* San Francisco, CA: Arcadia Publishing. 2009.

Superintendent's Annual Report of the Territorial Industrial School: June 30, 1911. Printed by The H.H. McNeil Co., Phoenix, Arizona.

"Swallowed Up." www3.gendisasters.com/arizona.

"Texas and Pacific Railway." www.tshaonline.org

Tellman, Barbara and Hadley, Diana. *Crossing Boundaries: An Environmental History of the Upper San Pedro River Watershed, Arizona and Sonora.* Tucson, Arizona: University of Arizona. Spring 2006.

Thomas, Bob. "Arizona Ranch 'Toughened Up' Young JFK." *Arizona Republic.* Jan. 17, 1988.

Tombstone Arizona History. https://tombstoneweb.com/history/

Travous, Ken. "Kartchner Caverns: A Gift of Nature." *Arizona Highways*, vol. 71, no. 9, September 1995. Phoenix, Arizona: Arizona Department of Transportation. pp. 4-13.

Trimble, Marshall. *Arizona Adventure.* Phoenix, Arizona: Golden West Publishers. 1982. pp. 139-140.

---. *Arizona: A Cavalcade of History.* Tucson, Arizona: Rio Nuevo Publishers. 2003.

Traywick, Ben T. "The Demise of Jack the Ripper." *San Pedro Valley News-Sun: Second Annual Historical Edition.* March 1972. p. 7.

Tucson and Tombstone General and Business Directory for 1883 and 1884. Includes Benson Directory, pp. 215-224. Tucson, Arizona: Cobler & Co. 1883.

Underhill, Lonnie E., ed. "The Tombstone Discovery: The Recollections of Ed Schieffelin & Richard Gird." *Arizona and the West: A Quarterly Journal of History.* Tucson: The University of Arizona Press. Spring, 1979. pp. 37-76.

"U.S. Route 80 in Arizona."
https://en.wikipedia.org/wiki/U.S._Route_80_in_Arizona

USGS. "Historic Earthquakes." www.earthquake.usgs.gov

US Treasury Bonds http://www.u-s-history.com/pages/h1674.htm *US Treasury Bonds*

U.S. War Bonds http://www.u-s-history.com/pages/h1682.htm *U.S. War Bonds*

Warne, Julie. "Three finally may move to cemetery." The San Pedro Valley Arts & Historical Society. Benson Tidbits.

Wilharm, Peter B. *Benson History.* www.bensonvisitorcenter.com

Wilson, R. Michael. *Crime & Punishment in Early Arizona.* Las Vegas, Nevada: Stagecoach Books, 2004.

"Women's Club - Early History." The San Pedro Valley Arts & Historical Society: Vertical File.

Works Progress Administration (WPA).
http://en.wikipedia/.org/wiki/Works_Progress_Administration.

Mary Lee Tiernan

BIBLIOGRAPHY

Section 2
Newspapers

Early newspapers generally did not include all the data used for bibliographic entries such as a headline or a byline. The articles were simply listed one after the other often with a thin line separating them. Sometimes, they were listed under a column name such as "News Briefs" or "Local Matters," sometimes not. There are no bibliographic "rules" covering the inclusion of such articles in standard bibliographic form. The only common data to all articles was the name of the newspaper and the date of publication. For newspaper articles used for this book from 1880 -1945, the names of newspapers are listed alphabetically followed by excerpts listed in chronological order.

Arizona Champion (Peach Springs, AZ 1883-1891) Excerpts:
    "Fire in Benson." Oct. 13, 1883.
    "Weekly Champion." Feb. 2, 1884.
    "Local Matters." May 17, 1884.
    (no title) Dec. 26, 1885.
    (no title) July 17, 1886.
Arizona Citizen (Tucson, AZ 1870-1880) Excerpts:
    (no title) Sept. 9, 1871.
    (no title) March 23, 1872.
    "San Pedro Station." Advertisement. Dec. 20, 1873.
    (no title) March 1, 1873.
    "From Tucson to Grant." Sept. 20, 1873.
    "Notice." Feb 6, 1875.
    (no title) Feb. 6, 1875.
    "San Pedro Station." Advertisement. Aug. 21, 1875.
    "San Pedro Station." Advertisement. Jan. 11, 1879.
    "Notice." Aug. 15, 1879.
    "New Bridge on the San Pedro." Aug. 22, 1879.
    "Tucson and Tombstone Stageline." Advertisement. Oct. 11, 1879.
    "Wednesday's Daily." Dec. 20, 1879.

Arizona Daily Orb (Bisbee, AZ 1989-1900) Excerpts:
  "The Grand Central Hotel." Advertisement. April 28, 1900.
Arizona Republican (Phoenix, AZ 18??-19??) Excerpts:
  (no title) Aug. 5, 1890.
Arizona Sentinel (Yuma, AZ 1872-1911) Excerpts:
  (no title) Aug. 27, 1881.
  (no title) Aug. 23, 1879.
Arizona Silver Belt (Globe City, AZ 1878-19??) Excerpts:
  "Sulpher Valley News." May 24, 1884.
  (no title) June 1, 1889.
  (no title) March 3, 1894.
  (no title) March 31, 1894.
  (no title) May 19, 1894.
  (no title) May 26, 1894.
  (no title) July 11, 1901.
  "Telephone Office Fire." Jan. 11, 1906.
  "Happy Jack Duel Victim." Dec. 9, 1906, p. 2.
  "Hotel Banks Is Burned." March 25, 1909.
Arizona Weekly Citizen (Tucson, AZ 1880-1901) Excerpts:
  "Business of Benson." Feb. 13, 1881.
  "The Stage Robbers." March 27, 1881.
  (no title) Aug. 21, 1881.
  "Top and Bottom Gang." Aug. 28, 1881.
  (no title) Aug. 28, 1881.
  (no title) Sept. 4, 1881.
  (no title) Sept. 11, 1881.
  "Personal Mention." Oct. 9, 1881.
  "Total Wreck Hotel." Advertisement. May 14, 1882.
  "The Result of Dr. Gregory's Visit to Benson." Aug. 6, 1882.
  "Benson Reduction Works." Aug. 13, 1882.
  "Benson." August 20, 1882.
  "Pacific Coast." Sept. 22, 1882.
  (no title) Dec. 31, 1882.
  "Worse Than Ever." April 8, 1883.
  "Hotel to Rent!" Advertisement. May 19, 1883.
  (no title) April 28, 1883.
  (no title) June 9, 1883.
  (no title) July 7, 1883.
  (no title) Aug. 4, 1883.

(no title) Aug. 25, 1883.
"Telegraph." Sept. 22, 1883.
"Benson Herself Again." Oct. 6, 1883.
"Local Intelligence." Oct. 20, 1883.
"Weekly Mining Review." Nov. 17, 1883.
"Benson and Its People." Jan. 5, 1884.
"Telegraph." May 3, 1884.
(no title) Oct. 17, 1885.
(no title) Dec. 13, 1884.
"Benson." Sept. 26, 1885.
"Benson Items." Feb. 13, 1886.
"Another Account." May 15, 1886.
"Fire in Benson." May 15, 1886.
"Benson." July 24, 1886.
"In Tucson." April 21, 1888.
(no Title) Dec. 30. 1893.
(no title) March 7, 1896.

Arizona Weekly Journal-Miner (Prescott, AZ 1885-1903) Excerpts:
"An Arizona Cloud Burst." Oct. 7, 1896.
"Nearly a Ghost Dance." May 4, 1892.

Arizona Weekly Star (Tucson, AZ 1879-1907) Excerpts:
(no title) April 1, 1880.

Benson News (Benson, AZ 1922-1928)
Microfilm read: Aug.19, 1927 – Aug. 17, 1928. Excerpts:
"Man Killed in Power Plant Explosion at Benson." Nov. 18, 1927.
"Caravan of Death 600 miles Long Is Nations Auto Story." Feb. 10, 1928.
Editorial. Feb 10, 1928.
"Clean Up Program." Feb. 24, 1928.
"Accident Results in Revelation." March 2, 1928.
"Tricks of the Trade." March 9, 1928.

The Benson Signal (Benson, AZ 1915-1921)
Microfilm read: July 10, 1015 – Dec. 29, 1917. Excerpts:
"Lost or Stolen." Dec. 4, 1915.
"Large Stage Installed at Auditorium." July 10, 1915.
"Local Items." July 10, 1915.
"Good Bill at the Rink Theater Tonight." August 21, 1915.
"Rink Theater To Open Next Saturday Night." August 14, 1915.
"Rink Theater." Advertisement. August 21, 1915.

"Lost on Desert Wright Walker Nearly Perishes." Sept. 25, 1915.
"Local Items." Aug. 7, 1915.
"Local Items." Sept. 18, 1915.
"Constable John Proffitt Makes Haul." Nov. 6, 1915.
"Prohibition Helps the Workingman Says Mining Delegate." Sept. 9, 1916.
"At the Movies." Nov. 13, 1915.
"Local Items." Dec. 4, 1915.
"Will Put On Moving Picture Show." Feb 12, 1916.
"Canning Factory for Benson." Feb. 19, 1916.
"Local Items." March 18, 1916.
"False Alarm." April 21, 1916.
"Local Items." May 12, 1916.
"Skating Exhibition." June 3, 1916.
"Local Items: Notice." June 17, 1916.
"Benson Cannery Ready for Work." Aug. 5, 1916.
Editorial. Sept. 23, 1916.
"Local Items." October 6, 1916.
"Local Items." Oct. 28, 1916.
"News Briefs." Jan. 1, 1917.
"Local Items." Jan. 27, 1917.
"Increasing Home Production." April 21, 1917.
"Local Items." May 26, 1917.
"Local Items: Notice." June 2, 1917.
"Local Items." June 9, 1917.
Editorial. June 17, 1917.
"Local Items." June 17 and June 24, 1916.
"Local Items." July 18, 1917.
"Local Items." Aug. 18, 1917.
"Local Items." Sept. 15, 1917.
"Lost or Stolen." Dec. 22, 1917.
"Victory Garden." July 5, 1919.
"Factors of Benson's Continued Growth." Jan. 3, 1920.

Bisbee Daily Review (Bisbee, AZ 1901-1971) Excerpts:
"Brick Making Begins at Benson." Dec. 15, 1901.
(no title) Dec. 22, 1901.
(no title) Jan. 14, 1902.
(no title) March 6, 1902.
"The Arizona Clay Manufacturing Company." March 11, 1902.

"Gambler Shoots Another at Benson Late Yesterday." May 3, 1902.
"Jury's Verdict." May 7, 1902.
"Shepard Keeps Still." May 9, 1902.
"Benson Brick Plant Burned." May 16, 1902.
"District Court Continues: Trial of Sheppard." June 13, 1902.
"Nothing New about the Escapes." Dec. 19, 1903.
Advertisement for Hotel Banks. March 16, 1904.
"$30,000 Fire in Benson." Nov. 12, 1904.
"Post Office Restored." Nov. 20, 1904.
"Mansion Hotel." Advertisement. Feb. 14, 1905.
"Franchise at Benson." August 24, 1905.
"Benson Water Co." Oct. 5, 1905.
"Mining Section: Editorial Correspondence." Oct. 8, 1905.
"Benson News." Oct. 21, 1905.
"Fire at Benson." Jan. 5, 1906.
"Shot Up Benson." March 30, 1906.
"Four Room House Destroyed in Benson." April 23, 1906.
"Man Is Killed in Saloon Row." Dec. 1, 1906.
(no title) Dec. 4, 1906.
"Preliminary Hearing Has Been Postponed." Dec. 6, 1906.
"Courthouse Notes from County's Capitol." Dec. 13, 1906.
"Four-Room House Destroyed in Benson." April 23, 1906.
"Brief City News." Jan. 11, 1907.
"Wheeler Gives Statement to Press." March 6, 1907.
"Injunction to Raise Some Question." August 29, 1907.
"Artesian Well for Benson School." Oct. 19, 1907.
"Fire Loss of $900." June 5, 1908.
"Banks Hotel Burned Sunday in Benson." March 23, 1909.
"Deputy Trask Shot by Unknown, Seriously Wounds Assailant." May 11, 1911.
"Trask Shot in Air to Frighten Smith." May 12, 1911.
"Court Reconvenes Calendar of Week Is Now Prepared." January 4, 1912.
"Storm Visits Benson with High Wind." July 8, 1919. p. 5.
"Station Completed." March 30, 1922, p. 3.

Cochise Review (Bisbee, AZ 1900-1901) Excerpts:
(no title) Oct. 10, 1900.
"The Water Discovery Shows the Possibilities of This Important Feature." August 20, 1900.

(no title) Nov. 13, 1900.
Cocoinino Sun (Flagstaff, AZ 1891-1891, 1898-1978) Excerpts:
  (no title) May 25, 1901.
  (no title) Nov. 30, 1901.
  (no title) May 19, 1911.
Cocoinino Weekly Sun (Flagstaff, AZ 1891-1896) Excerpts:
  (no title) May 17, 1894.
  (no title) Aug. 9, 1894.
  "Glacier in Arizona." Oct. 22, 1896.
Daily Arizona Silver Belt (Globe, AZ 1906-1929) Excerpts:
  "Copper Production of AZ Mines." July 24, 1908.
The Daily Tombstone (Tombstone, AZ 1885-1887) Excerpts:
  (no title) Sept. 16, 1885.
  "Benson Burnt." May 10, 1886.
  (no title) May 13, 1886.
  "Benson Notes." July 19, 1886.
  "District Court." Nov. 19, 1886.
  "Sheriff's Sale." Dec. 4, 1886.
  "Benson Tid Bits." March 27, 1887.
Daily Tombstone Epitaph (Tombstone, AZ 1885-1887) Excerpts:
  "Benson Items." Jan. 21, 1886.
  "Benson Items." Feb. 7, 1886.
  "Notice for Publication." Feb. 28, 1886.
  "Notice." May 23, 1886.
  (no title) March 3, 1887.
Graham Guardian (Safford, AZ 1895-1923) Excerpts:
  (no title) June 7, 1901.
  "A Terrible Flood." Oct. 9, 1896.
  "A Fatal Shooting." May 9, 1902.
  "Benson News." Dec. 11, 1903.
Mohave County Miner (Mineral Park, AZ 1882-1918) Excerpts:
  (no title) April 7, 1888.
  (no title) June 8, 1889.
The Oasis (Arizola, AZ 1893-1920) Excerpts:
  "School Census." July 26, 1894.
  "Virginia Hotel." Advertisement. Oct. 18, 1894.
  "Benson Items." Aug. 7, 1897.
  "Benson Items." May 7, 1898.
  "The Passing of East Benson." Oct. 15, 1898

"Benson Items." Dec. 31, 1898.
"Benson Items." August 26, 1899.
"News Briefs." 1903.
"The Benson Smelter." Dec. 10, 1904.
"Benson Smelter May Work." August 11, 1906.
"Arizona News." Sept. 19, 1908.

The San Pedro Valley News (Benson, AZ 1928-1958)
Microfilm read: Jan. 2, 1931 – Dec. 31, 1948. Excerpts:
Editorial. Feb. 6, 1931.
"Throw Away Day." April 17, 1931.
Editorial comment. March 6, 1931.
"Youth Killed by Fall from Freight Train." June 12, 1931.
"News Briefs." Sept. 29, 1931.
"Gila Monster Is Victorious in Battle with Rattlesnake." Oct. 16, 1931.
"Night Prowler Is Caught." June 10, 1932.
(no title) Dec. 2, 1932.
"Personal." Jan. 6, 1933.
"Apache Powder Co. Has Never Cut Pay." Sept. 1, 1933, p.1.
"Recovery Everywhere." Sept. 22, 1933.
"The Meanest Thief Found in Benson." Jan. 5, 1934.
"For Rent." March, 1934.
"Thief Gets Voting Booth." Sept. 21, 1934.
"Paralysis Causes Schools to Close." Oct. 5, 1934.
"News Briefs." Oct. 19, 1934.
"The Neighborhood." Nov. 1, 1935.
"For Rent." Nov. 1935.
(no title) Jan. 17, 1936.
"Quarantine Is Declared for Measles and Mumps." Feb. 21, 1936.
(no title) March 27, 1936.
"For Rent." April 3, 1936.
"For Rent." April 24, 1936.
"News Briefs." Feb. 5, 1937.
Editorial comment. Aug. 20, 1937.
Personal item. Sept. 10, 1937.
"For Rent." Dec. 3, 1937.
(no title) Feb. 11, 1938.
"News Briefs." Oct. 28, 1938.
Editorial. April 7, 1939.

"Personal." July 7, 1939.
"Building Fences to Keep Out Cattle." Oct. 20, 1939.
"Seen and Heard Around Town," Jan. 12, 1940.
"Earthquake Felt Here in Benson Saturday Night." May 24, 1940.
"A Little Safety Talk." Aug. 23, 1940.
Sunday school announcement. Aug. 23, 1940.
Letter from Louis Robinson. July 19, 1940.
"This Week in Defense." November 29, 1940.
"This Week in Defense." March 14, 1941.
"This Week in Defense." August 8, 1941.
Help Wanted Advertisement. October 3, 1941.
"U.S. Declares War on Germany, Italy; Sink Jap Ship at Wake." December 12, 1941, p. 1.
"Seen and Heard Around Town." May 8, 1942.
Letter from Louis Robinson. Published Jan 2, 1942; dated Dec. 22, 1941.
"This Week in Defense." Aug. 8, 1942.
"Dances - Rodeo - Racing on Annual Program." August 28, 1942.
"$200 Would Make Him a Capitalist Rodeo Sponsor Thot (*thought*)." August 28, 1942.
"This Week in Defense." Sept. 11, 1942.
"It Is a Pleasing Picture for Mrs. Rosa M. Schwab." Sept. 18, 1942.
"Seen and Heard Around Town." Jan. 1, 1943.
"Seen and Heard Around Town." Aug. 20, 1943.
Advertisement. May 19, 1944.
"Benson Children Nearly Mob Santa Claus." Dec. 29, 1944.
Letter to Senator Carl Hayden. June 1, 1945.
"Seen and Heard Around Town." June 15, 1945.

Tombstone Daily Prospector (Tombstone, AZ 1887-1891) Excerpts:
"Virginia Hotel." Advertisement. Dec. 2, 1890.
"Virginia Hotel." Advertisement. Jan. 1, 1899.
(no title) Jan. 24, 1889.
(no title) Feb. 4, 1889.

Tombstone Epitaph (Tombstone, AZ 1880-1882) Excerpts:
"Tucson Topics." Jan. 23, 1882.
"The Chinese Must Go." April 24, 1882.
"Communications." May 13, 1882.
"Benson, June 4, 1882." June 10, 1882.
"The Benson Rustlers." July 29, 1882.

(no title) Oct. 7, 1882.
"The School at Benson." Nov. 4, 1882.
The Tombstone Weekly Epitaph (Tombstone, AZ 1882-1887) Excerpts:
"Benson Happenings." June 24, 1882.
"Cochise County Census." July 15, 1882.
Tombstone Epitaph (Tombstone, AZ 1887-current) Excerpts:
(no title) Dec. 10, 1887.
"Gill-Coleman." Jan. 7, 1888.
"Benson Mining and Smelting Co." Jan. 21, 1888.
(no title) Feb. 18, 1888.
(no title) August 1, 1889.
"Roll of Honor." Dec. 7, 1889.
(no title) July 5, 1890.
"Benson Mining and Smelting Co." Feb. 1, 1891.
"A Grand Reception." April 26, 1891.
"A Correct Report." April 26, 1891.
(no title) May 17, 1891.
"Grand Central Hotel." Advertisement. Dec. 20. 1891.
(no title) June 7, 1893.
(no title) Oct. 4, 1893.
(no title) Dec. 24, 1893.
(no title) June 17, 1894.
(no title) June 24, 1894.
"Benson Bits." July 8, 1894.
"Benson Bits." Aug. 12, 1894.
"Washed Out." Aug. 26, 1894.
"The Railroad." Aug. 26, 1894.
"Benson Bits." Sept. 2, 1894.
"Benson Bits." Sept. 16, 1894.
"Benson to Bisbee." Sept. 30, 1894.
"Benson Bits." Oct. 14, 1894.
(no title) Oct. 28, 1894.
(no title) Nov. 11, 1894.
(no title) Nov. 18, 1894.
(no title) Feb. 3, 1895.
Advertisement carriage prices. Nov. 10, 1895.
"Benson School House." Sept. 25, 1898.
(no title) July 2, 1899.
"County Records - Deeds." July 16, 1899.

(no title) August 13, 1899.
(no title) June 2, 1901.
(no title) Sept. 15, 1901.
"A Killing at Benson Yesterday." May 4, 1902.
"Disastrous Fire at Benson Yesterday." July 1, 1906.
"Man Is Killed in Saloon Row." Dec. 1, 1906.
(no title) Dec. 4, 1906.
"A Fatal Killing Reported at Benson." March 3, 1907.
"Ranger Wheeler Resting Easy." March 3, 1907.
(no title) June 7, 1908.
"Constable Frank Trask Murdered by a Tramp." May 14, 1911.
"Prisoner Brought to Tombstone Today." June 4, 1911.
(No title) Feb. 25, 1912.
"Princely Gift to Benson School Dist." April 5, 1914.

Weekly Arizona Citizen (Tucson, AZ 1880-1880) Excerpts:
"Auction Sale of Lots!" June 19. 1880.
(no title) July 10, 1880.
"Mysterious Disappearance." Oct. 2, 1880.
"Hail to the Chief." October 30, 1880.
"Another Murder." Nov. 13, 1880.
"That Murdered Man." Nov. 13, 1880.
(no title) Nov. 27, 1880.

Weekly Phoenix Herald (Phoenix, AZ 1882-1896) Excerpts:
"The Fire Sufferers." Sept. 20, 1883.

The Weekly Arizona Miner (Prescott, AZ 1868-1873) Excerpts:
"The Coming Town in Southern Arizona." April 20, 1880.
(no title) Aug. 7, 1885.

Suggested Reading about another town founded during the settlement of the West in the 1880s. Sunland, originally named Monte Vista, began during the Land Boom of the 1880s. Monte Vista failed to develop and is listed in some histories as a ghost town. However, the village did grow and prosper in the hands of the settlers who stayed. Although details are specific to Sunland, its history is similar to that of many small towns that were founded and developed after the transcontinental railroad opened the West for settlement.

The Early History of Sunland, California:

Vol. 1 *Hotels for the Hopeful*
Vol. 2 *The Roscoe Robbers and the Sensational Train Robbery of 1894*
Vol. 3 *The Parson and His Cemetery*
Vol. 4 *From Crackers to Coal Oil*
Vol. 5 *He Never Came Home*
Vol. 6 *Lancasters Lake*
Vol. 7 *Living in Big Tujunga Canyon*
Vol. 8 *From Whence They Came*

Individual volumes sold separately. Descriptions of each volume can be found on **https://www.maryleetiernan.com/History**.

The Early History of Sunland, California: Vol. 1-8

Made in the USA
Las Vegas, NV
05 August 2021